LETTS POCKET GUIDE TO

MAMMALS

The most common species
of European mammals
described and illustrated in colour

Eleanor Lawrence and Ruth Lindsay

Distribution map

- Commonly found in these regions
- ○ Partial distribution only
- * Other species on page commonly found in these regions

Front cover illustration: Hedgehog

This edition first published in 1993
by Charles Letts & Co Ltd
Letts of London House
Parkgate Road
London SW11 4NQ

'Letts' is a registered trademark of
Charles Letts & Co Limited

This edition produced under licence by
Malcolm Saunders Publishing Ltd, London

A CIP catalogue record for this book is available from the British Library

ISBN 1 85238 392 5

Printed in Spain by Graficas Reunidas

Contents

Introduction

The sight of a mammal in the wild, especially a large one, gives most people more of a thrill than the sight of any other kind of animal. Mammals generally are more difficult to find than for example, butterflies and birds, and quite a few are very rare, inhabiting wild and inaccessible areas. Often shy creatures, some species tend to come out only at dawn or dusk or even late at night, which makes them difficult to catch sight of and identify. You will generally only find clues to their presence, such as burrows, holes, tracks in mud or snow, droppings, broken branches or the remains of a meal.

This book describes more than 130 European mammals. Most are indigenous and only a few species have been introduced from elsewhere. We have included all the mammals of Central and Western Europe, with the exception of a few species with extremely limited distribution. Some of the animals included will be very familiar. Others only survive today in the wilder areas of forests and mountains, but you may come across them in national parks or other protected areas.

Some mammals adapt well to changes in their living conditions and can benefit from a man-made environment. However, in Europe, many species are in constant danger from the loss of their habitat, from intensive farming and from indiscriminate hunting. Some are now protected in many countries. So, if you find a hide, a nest or a burrow, respect it and leave it alone.

How to use this book

We have divided the book into eight sections based primarily on the biology of the mammals themselves. The sections are: **Insectivores**; **Bats**; **Carnivores**; **Rodents**; **Rabbits and Hares**; **Hoofed Mammals**; **Primates** and **Marine Mammals**. Each section is indicated by a different colour band at the top of each page. Within each section similar mammals are grouped together as described in the *Guide to Identification*, and each group has its own symbol, so that comparison is made easy. To identify your mammal, first decide to which section it belongs, using the information and symbols in the *Guide to Identification* which follows.

Guide to Identification

Page numbers given at the end of each section will enable you to turn directly to the relevant section of the book.

INSECTIVORES

Insectivores are a heterogeneous group with two main common features: all have four five-fingered feet and all feed on larvae, insects, worms etc., as well as vegetable matter.

Hedgehogs are the only European mammals covered with short sharp spines. **14**

Shrews look like mice, but are usually smaller. They have soft fur, a long whiskery snout and tiny round eyes. Many of them are quite ferocious, defending themselves fearlessly against predators and attacking prey as big as they are. **15**

Moles live underground and are rarely seen. Often, the only signs of their presence are the mounds or ridges of earth thrown up above ground by their tunnelling operations. They have thick fur, tiny eyes often covered with skin and spade-like forelimbs for digging. The Desman, a relative of the Mole, of which only one species still exists in Western Europe, is a good swimmer with a long mobile snout. **21**

BATS

The only true flying mammals, these animals are nocturnal. They have small furry bodies, hairless wings and complicated echo location devices in ears or on noses for avoiding obstacles in the dark and for locating insects on the wing. They emit a very high-pitched sound, imperceptible to the human ear. **23**

CARNIVORES

These are traditionally the meat-eating animals, the predators, and many of them are hunters and killers. Others prefer a more varied diet of berries and nuts as well as hunting prey animals. A characteristic feature is the big canines or eye teeth and they all have five toes on the front feet; the number of toes on the hind feet may be four or five.

Bears are large, heavily built carnivores, shambling in their movements, with large short legs and tails. They walk with the whole of each foot touching the ground so that the five sharp claws and the heel show in their tracks, but can also stand upright on their back legs. They are more omnivorous in their diets than many carnivores and their canines are poorly developed. **37**

Wolves and **Foxes** are dog-like, with pointed muzzles, pointed ears and long legs. They are effective hunters and killers with well-developed canines. These animals are the most vocal of the carnivores, making a variety of sounds from howling to whining and snarling. Some are pack animals while others are solitary. **38**

Raccoons are medium-sized carnivores, with long furry tails and arched backs. They are omnivorous and have poorly developed canines. They are good climbers. **43**

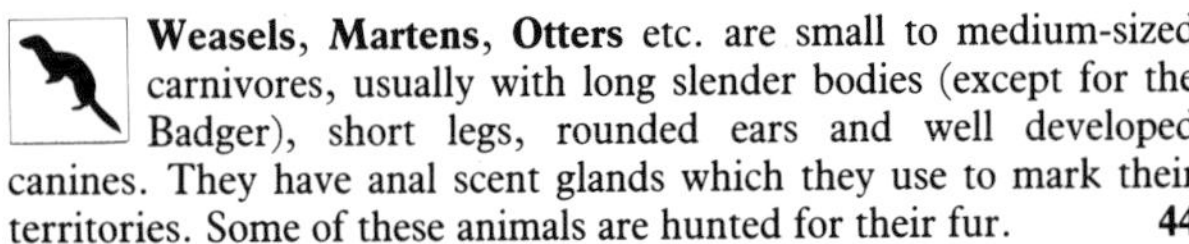

Weasels, **Martens**, **Otters** etc. are small to medium-sized carnivores, usually with long slender bodies (except for the Badger), short legs, rounded ears and well developed canines. They have anal scent glands which they use to mark their territories. Some of these animals are hunted for their fur. **44**

The **Civet** and the **Mongoose** look like Weasels but have a long pointed tail and rougher fur. **54**

Cats seem to be the most specialized of the Carnivores: they have strong canines and feed exclusively on meat. They look like larger versions of our domestic cat. They have small heads and binocular vision, pointed ears, silky fur and long legs and retractable claws on their feet. **56**

RODENTS

Rodents have characteristic gnawing incisor teeth at the front of the jaws. These are covered with hard enamel on the front surface so that the front of the teeth wears away more slowly than the back, thus ensuring a sharp cutting edge. Rodents have no canines so there is a gap between the incisors and the grinding teeth. Most Rodents have four toes on each fore limb and five on the back.

Squirrels, **Sousliks** and **Marmots** are medium-sized rodents. Tree Squirrels have bushy tails which curl over their backs. All but the Flying Squirrel are active during the day. **59**

Dormice are exclusively nocturnal. These small mammals have big eyes and a hairy tail. **64**

Voles and **Lemmings** are small and squat with thick silky fur which almost hides their tiny ears. They have short hairy tails. This group includes the Hamster and the Mole Rat. **67**

Rats and **Mice** are small to medium-sized rodents. They have short fur, large ears and their long tails are hairless or covered in short hair. Even though it is related to the Mole, the Muskrat is included in this group because of its scaly tail. **78**

Some other large Rodents, like the **Beaver**, the **Coypu** and the **Porcupine** are quite dissimilar both in appearance and habits. **87**

RABBITS AND HARES

Like rodents these mammals have front teeth (incisors) adapted for gnawing. However they have four incisors in the upper jaw, one pair behind the other and two incisors in the lower. Medium in size, they have long narrow ears, long powerful hind limbs and a short fluffy tail. **90**

HOOFED MAMMALS

With the exception of pigs, all these large mammals have long legs and hoofed feet with only two functional toes, together forming a cloven hoof, and bear antlers or horns. Deer have bony antlers; cows, goats and sheep have horns. They are herbivores and have a pad of hard cartilage at the front of the jaws for nipping off grasses and other vegetation. The back teeth have complicated crowns and are used for grinding the tough plant food. These animals are ruminants. **93**

Pigs have the same two functional toes, but two other toes are present much higher up the leg. They are more heavily-built than the rest, with sparse hair and short legs; they do not have horns. Their faces end in disc-like snouts which they use for digging and they have well-developed canines which form tusks which they also use for self-defence. Pigs are not ruminants. **103**

PRIMATES

This group includes, among others, **monkeys** and **humans**. Only one species (apart from Man) lives in Europe: the Barbary Ape. **104**

MARINE MAMMALS

Seals have streamlined bodies, and a thick layer of fat which acts as thermal insulation. They have short fur and both fore and hind limbs have been modified to become flippers. **105**

Dolphins, **Porpoises** and **Whales** have streamlined fish-shaped bodies, with front limbs modified into flippers, no hind limbs and a tail ending in a horizontal fluke. These marine mammals can be divided into two main groups: toothed whales (dolphins, porpoises and some whales) and baleen whales whose jaws have horny plates or baleen which act as a filter and retain the food.

Making a positive identification

Once you have decided on the section to which your mammal belongs, you can turn to the pages on which the individual species are described and illustrated. The size of the mammal, from the tip of the head to the base of the tail, is given in the coloured band at the top of the page; the length of the tail is then given separately. These sizes are average; if you have the chance to measure a specimen don't be surprised at quite large variations.

Four boxes provide information which make positive identification possible. The first box provides details of features or combinations of features which, together with the illustration, enable you to identify your mammal. The second box gives you supplementary information on the biology of the animal. Habitat and distribution are given in the third box and a distribution map is provided for quick reference. Finally the fourth box indicates some of the species with which this mammal might be confused.

Characteristic features

Included in this box is a general indication of the shape and size of the mammal; its fur, colour and markings; and any other characteristic features like the shape of its tail or ears, presence of horns, flippers etc.

Biology and habits

In this box you will find details of the animal's habits to help in identification; the time of day at which the particular species is most likely to be seen; whether it is solitary or lives in groups; and whether it makes a burrow or den. Feeding habits are also given. Many mammals leave signs and traces to indicate their presence, although the animal itself may not be seen. Tracks are included in the illustration but where large groups of mammals leave very similar tracks (e.g. shrews), these are shown only once.

Habitat and distribution

There is a wide variety of climate and geography in Europe, from the cold northern tundra to the warmth of the Mediterranean. The distribution maps will tell you at a glance whether or not the animal lives in a particular area. The third box gives detailed information on habitat and distribution. A mammal may not be common, or even present, throughout the whole of its range, being confined to those areas within the range with a suitable habitat.

Similar species

Finally in the fourth box are given some of the mammals with which this one might be confused. Those similar species printed in **heavy** type are illustrated, either as a featured mammal or in the pages of *Other Species*.

Other species

Some large groups of mammals include very similar species, as in the Bats, Voles and Shrews. In these cases, several less common species or species with limited distribution are grouped on the same page.

Specimen page

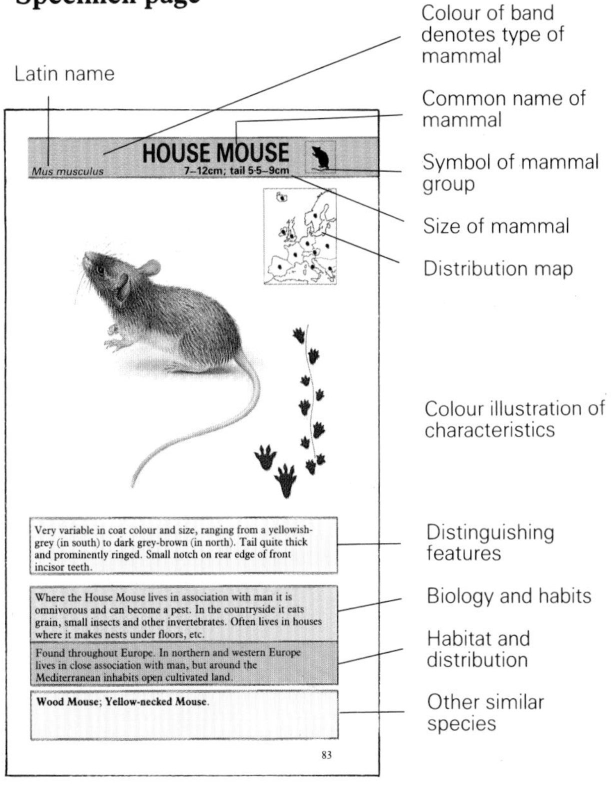

COMMON HEDGEHOG

20–30cm; tail 2–4cm *Erinaceus europaeus*

One of the most familiar small mammals. It has short sharp stiff spines over back and sides, short legs and a pointed snout. Rolls up in a spiky ball when frightened or attacked. Hibernates in winter in a nest of dry grass or leaves.

Nocturnal, coming out soon after dusk and often revealing its presence by a snuffling noise while searching for food. It eats insects, grubs, small frogs, lizards and young mice, as well as berries and other plant food.

Found in many different habitats from heaths to woodland throughout western Europe and southern Scandinavia. Common in gardens and cultivated land.

Replaced by the similar *E. concolor* in Greece and eastern Europe. The Algerian Hedgehog on the Med. coast of France and Spain has longer legs, larger ears, and does not hibernate.

COMMON SHREW

Sorex araneus
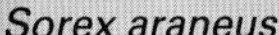

5·5–8·5cm; tail 3·5–5·5cm

A relatively big shrew weighing between 4–16g, with a long tail, long pointed mobile snout, velvety brownish-black fur on back and paler undersides. The small ears are hidden by fur and the teeth have brown tips.

Active at all times, usually searching for food. Feeds on earthworms and other small invertebrates, and also takes larger carrion. Makes a nest of leaves and grass in dense vegetation.

Found in a wide range of habitats throughout Europe, but absent from Ireland, the Mediterranean islands and most of Spain.

Pygmy Shrew (*S. minutus*) is paler and smaller. The similarly sized Lesser White-toothed Shrew (*C. suaveolens*) and other similar shrews have uniformly white teeth and visible ears.

PYGMY SHREW

4·5–6cm; tail 3·5–4·5cm *Sorex minutus*

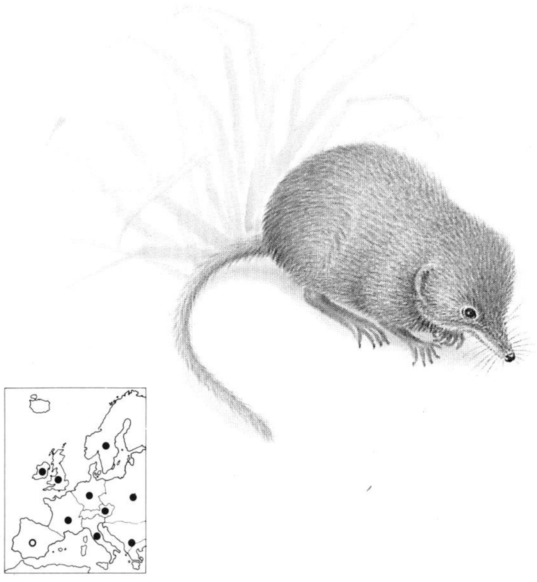

A small shrew weighing 2–7g. Brownish velvety fur on back with pale undersides. Ears hidden under fur. Tail pinched in at root and slightly bushy in young animals. Brown tips to teeth.

Active at all times, deep in vegetation, feeding mainly on spiders, beetles and other small invertebrates. A good swimmer and climber.

Common in a wide range of habitats, especially heath and damp swampy ground. All Europe except central and southern Iberia and Med. islands, but only in hills and mountains in south.

The **Common Shrew** (*S. araneus*) is larger and darker with tail not pinched in at root. **Savi's Pygmy Shrew** (*Suncus etruscus*) has all-white teeth and is even smaller.

WATER SHREW

Neomys fodiens **6·5–9·5cm; tail 5–8cm**

∗1

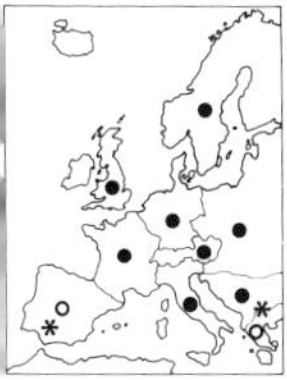

The largest shrew in Europe, weighing 10–20g. It has a dense black waterproof coat on back, and white undersides. Stiff bristles on underside of tail and hindfeet help it steer while swimming.

Active day and night. An excellent swimmer and diver, spending much of its life in water, but is also agile on land. It feeds mainly in the water, on insects, water snails, small fish etc.

Beside water, especially slow-flowing rivers and small streams. Throughout Europe except Ireland and most of Iberian peninsula.

Miller's Water Shrew (*N. anomalus*) (**1**) is similar in colour but slightly smaller and the bristles on feet and tail are less prominent. It is also found in damp places away from water.

LESSER WHITE-TOOTHED SHREW

5·5–8cm; tail 2·5–4·5cm *Crocidura suaveolens*

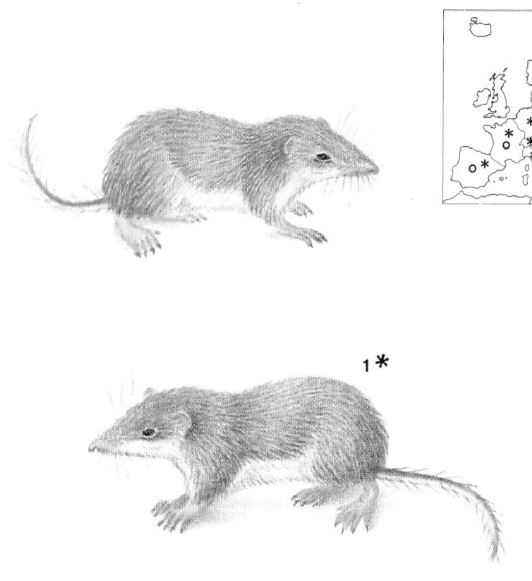

A smallish shrew weighing 3–7g. It has greyish-brown velvety fur on back gradually shading to paler undersides. Teeth are completely white and ears are visible.

Active at all times, feeding on insects, grubs and other small invertebrates. If a female with young is disturbed she may lead them away in a line, each holding in its teeth the base of the tail of the one in front.

Open land, sometimes in haystacks and barns in winter. Likes drier, warmer areas than other shrews. S. Europe north to central France and Germany, Sicily, Sardinia, Scilly Isles.

Greater White-toothed Shrew (1) is larger and darker and found also in N. France and Germany. ***C. leucodon***: sharply defined markings, eastwards from E. France.

OTHER SHREWS

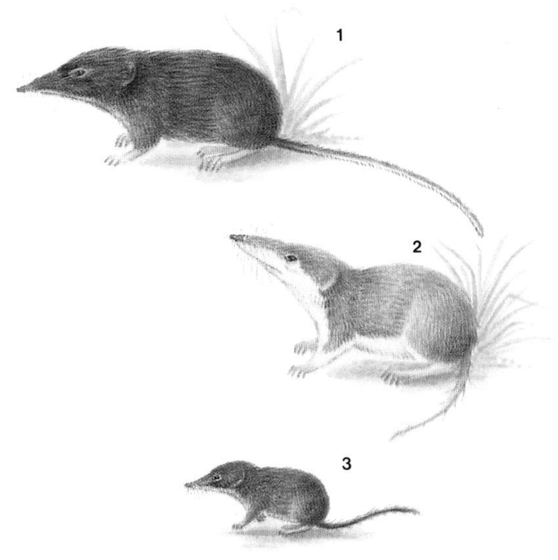

Alpine Shrew (*Sorex alpinus*) (**1**)
–7·5cm.
Slate grey above, slightly lighter below, tail as long as head and body. In Alps and mountains of entral Europe, in coniferous forest near water.

Bicoloured White-toothed Shrew (*Crocidura leucodon*) (**2**)
·5–8·5cm.
harply demarcated white underparts and brown back. Shortish tail, darker above than below. Makes 'caravans' of young, each holding the tail of the one in front, if nest is disturbed. Grassland, woodland, hedgerows, in central and eastern Europe; not found in Iberia, British Isles or most of France.

Pygmy White-toothed Shrew (*Suncus etruscus*) (**3**) 3·5–4·5cm.
The smallest shrew, hardly bigger than a large beetle, but preying on insects like grasshoppers and crickets. Mediterranean lowlands and W. France in grassland, scrub and gardens, under stones and logs.

OTHER SHREWS

Soricidae

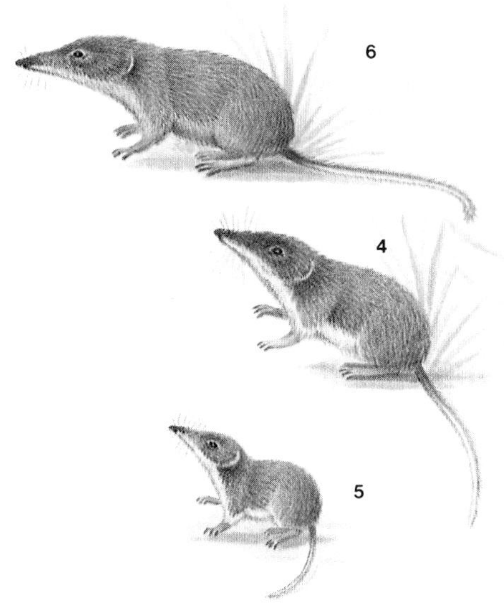

Laxmann's Shrew (*Sorex caecutiens*) (**4**) 5–7cm.
Intermediate in size between Common and Pygmy Shrews. Tail clearly tufted when young. Forests and tundra in Scandinavia eastwards.

Least Shrew (*S. minutissimus*) (**5**) 3·5–4·5cm.
Very small, short hind feet distinguishing it from the young of other shrews. Shortish tail. Damp coniferous forest in Scandinavia eastwards.

Dusky Shrew (*S. sinalis*) (**6**) 6–8cm.
A large shrew, grey brown on back with grey underparts. Damp coniferous forest in Scandinavia eastwards.

COMMON MOLE

Talpa europaea **10–15cm; tail 2·5cm**

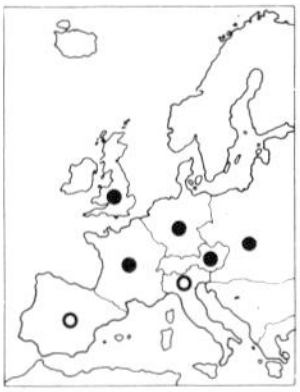

A burrowing animal living mainly underground, with broad spade-like front feet adapted for digging. Covered in dense velvety black fur except for snout and feet. Eyes tiny and often covered with a soft skin.

Indicates its presence by molehills thrown up along its tunnel system. Mainly nocturnal, rarely emerging above ground and feeds on insects, grubs and earthworms it finds while digging. Does not live in very damp or sandy ground.

Relatively common on cultivated land, pastures, gardens, golf-courses, etc. Throughout Europe except extreme south and north and Ireland.

T. caeca (Iberia, Med. coast, N. Italy) smaller. *T. romana* (SW. Italy) only distinguishable by its skull. **Mole-rats**: light brown with rat-like front feet.

PYRENEAN DESMAN

11–13·5cm; tail 13–15cm *Galemys pyrenaicus*

A mole-sized animal with a long mobile snout and webbed back feet. The long, sparsely haired tail is flattened towards the end and bears a musk gland at its base, producing a powerful and offensive scent.

A burrowing animal, excavating underground passages. It is also a good swimmer. Feeds on water and on land, on aquatic insects and their larvae, worms, and small fish, frogs and mammals.

Lives beside small mountain streams in valleys in the Pyrenees and mountains of northern Spain and Portugal.

None.

HORSESHOE BATS

Rhinolophidae

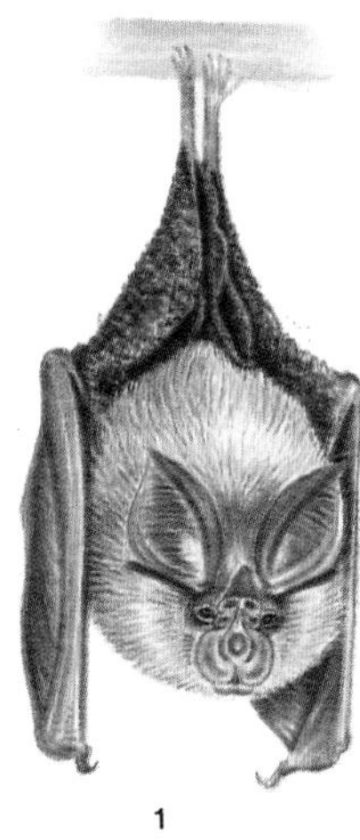

1

2

Greyish bats, pale underneath, with pointed ears and a complicated horseshoe-shaped fold of skin around the nose. The shape of this 'nose-leaf' is used to identify the different species. Flying mainly at night, from early evening onwards. They are all warmth loving and most common in southern Europe.

The **Greater Horseshoe Bat** (*Rhinolophus ferrumequinum*) (**1**) is the largest (body length 5·5–6·5cm; wingspan 35cm), and has a reddish tinge to the fur on its back. It has been found in north-western France and south-west Britain.

The **Lesser Horseshoe Bat** (*R. hipposideros*) (**2**) is tiny (around 4cm; wingspan 20–22cm). Its range reaches northwestern France and southwest Britain and Ireland.

Both form quite large summer colonies in caves and deserted buildings, and hibernate in winter, hanging from the roofs of caves with their wings wrapped around them.

OTHER HORSESHOE BATS

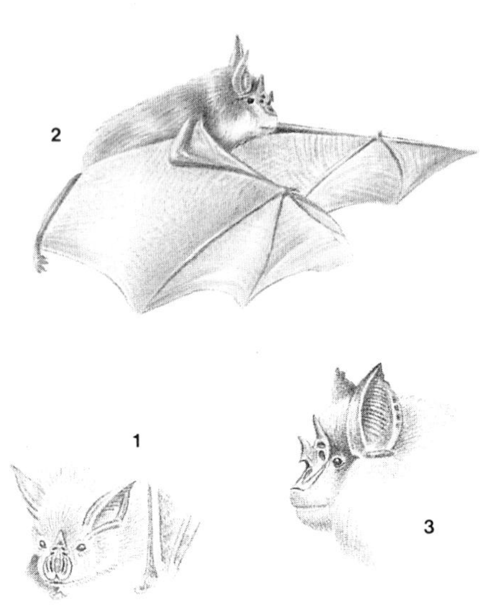

The **Mediterranean Horseshoe Bat** (*Rhinolophus euryale*) (**1**), is a southern European species, between the Greater and Lesser Horseshoe Bats in size. It forms very large summer colonies of up to 1000 individuals. It does not completely enfold itself with its wings when resting.

Mehely's Horseshoe Bat (*R. mehelyi*) (**2**) is a large horseshoe bat, pale in colour, with large ears. It lives mainly in caves in the Mediterranean region.

Blasius Horseshoe Bat (*R. blasii*) (**3**) is very similar to the Mediterranean Horseshoe Bat and is best distinguished by the shape of the nose-leaf. It lives mainly in caves in southeastern Europe.

WHISKERED BAT

Myotis mystacinus **4–4·5cm; wingspan 21–25cm**

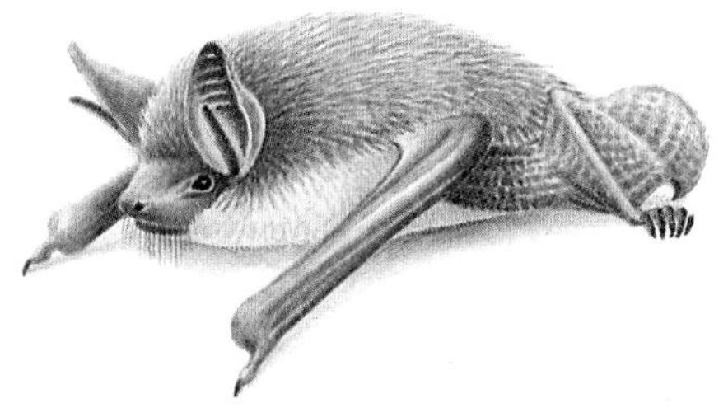

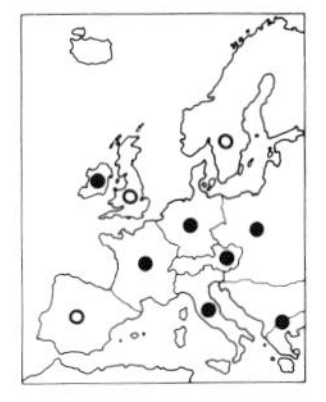

Small bat with dark wings, nose and ears, dark greyish-brown fur on back, paler undersides and a row of stiff hairs above the corner of the mouth. The slender, pointed tragus reaches slightly less than halfway up the ear.

Sometimes flies by day in spring and autumn, but main flights are just after sunset and before sunrise. Takes insects in the air and from twigs and leaves. Emits a low buzzing squeak. Seen in meadows around woods and around buildings.

Occurs throughout Europe except parts of Spain, Denmark, Scotland and extreme north. Summer roosts are in hollow trees and deserted buildings. Hibernates in caves, cellars, etc.

The rarer Brandt's Bat is identical in size and appearance and has the same range. It can only be distinguished by details of its teeth and the shape of its penis.

NATTERER'S BAT

4–5cm; wingspan 28cm *Myotis nattereri*

1 *

Greyish-brown bat, white below, with oval translucent pink ears. Tragus ⅔ length of ear. Thick fringe of stiff hairs along edge of wing between tail and hind leg.

Seen in woodland, towns, villages on warm calm nights. Flies in early evening and hunts throughout night, emitting an audible shrill continuous squeak. Flies slowly and steadily; catches moths in flight and picks insects off leaves.

Throughout Europe except most of Scandinavia, Sardinia, Greece and Yugoslavia. Roosts in hollow trees, nestboxes; in winter squeezes into cracks in caves and old buildings.

Geoffroy's Bat (1) (C. & S. Europe) forms large colonies, is same size but reddish brown with different shaped ears. Other *Myotis* species are also distinguishable by their ears.

GREATER MOUSE-EARED BAT

Myotis myotis **6·5–8·5cm; wingspan 36–45cm**

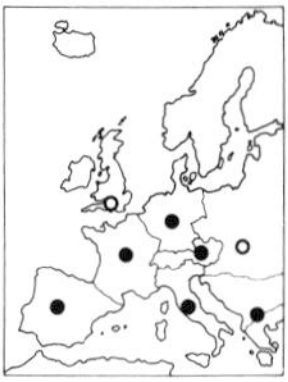

1

2

One of the commonest and largest European bats. Fur mid-brown on back with whitish underside. Like all mouse-eared bats it has large ears. Tragus slender and pointed.

In summer, forms very large breeding colonies in caves or buildings; in winter, individuals hibernate in caves. Flies well after dark, in open woodland where it catches ground beetles as well as flying insects.

Throughout Europe except Scandinavia; rarely recorded in Britain.

The **Lesser Mouse-eared Bat (1)** (S. Europe) is similar, with narrower ears, often roosts with *M. myotis*. **Bechstein's Bat (2)** (not in S. Europe) is smaller, with longer ears.

DAUBENTON'S BAT

4–5cm; wingspan 25cm *Myotis daubentoni*

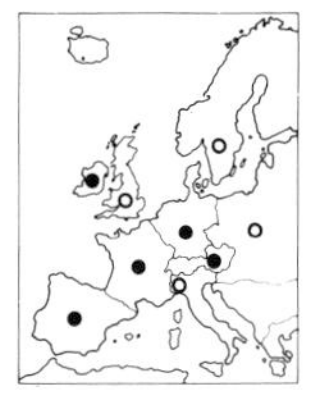

A small bat with relatively short ears and large feet. Fur dark reddish-brown on back, paler below. Tragus pointed with a convex back edge.

Associated with water where it hunts low over surface, taking insects from the water. Emerges from roost after a long period of squeaking but emits no audible sound while hunting.

Quite common over most of Europe except extreme north, Greece, most of Italy. Forms summer colonies in holes in trees, in tunnels, under bridges, etc. Hibernates singly.

The **Long-fingered Bat** (Med. coast & Italy) is greyer with larger feet. The rare Pond Bat (NE. France, Holland, Germany eastwards) raises its wings high above body when turning.

COMMON PIPISTRELLE 

Pipistrellus pipistrellus **3·5–5cm; wingspan 20–25cm**

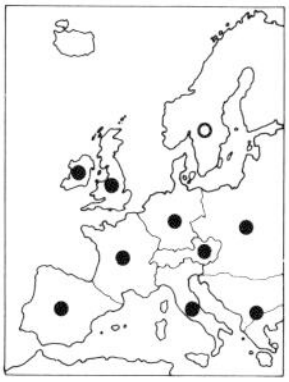

Europe's smallest bat, weighing only 3g at the end of hibernation. Reddish fur on back, paler beneath. It has narrow wings with a distinctive lobe of skin on outer edge of elongated 'thumb' of hind leg. Tragus short and blunt.

Flies soon after dusk and before dawn, emitting an audible rapid ticking sound. Summer breeding colonies in attics, etc. reveal themselves by noisy squeaking from the young. Catches insects in the air.

Common throughout Europe south of 60 °N in a wide range of habitats from woodland to towns and villages. Hibernates in caves, cellars and old houses.

Other European pipistrelles: slightly larger and differ in colour and details of teeth (see next page). Pipistrelles are distinguishable from *Myotis* bats by shape of ears and tragus.

OTHER PIPISTRELLES

Vespertilionidae

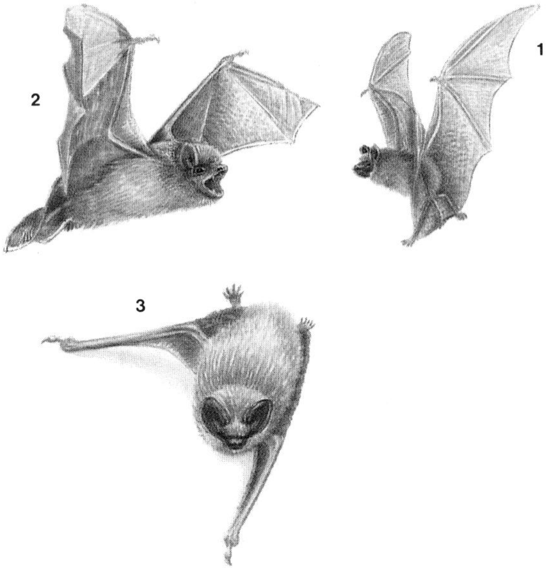

Nathusius's Pipistrelle (*Pipistrellus nathusii*) **(1)** Slightly frosted appearance and less uniform colour than the Common Pipistrelle. Broader wing. The small tooth between canine and large premolar does not overlap adjacent teeth. Most common in eastern Europe, in woodland.

Kuhl's Pipistrelle (*P. kuhli*) **(2)** Very similar to Common Pipistrelle but usually lighter in colour. White edge to extreme hind margin of wing. Small tooth behind upper canine, tiny and hardly visible from outside. Southern Europe and western France in habitats similar to Common Pipistrelle.

Savi's Pipistrelle (*P. savii*) **(3)** Similar to *P. nathusii* but with a definite contrast between dark upper parts and paler underside. A frosted appearance due to light tips to the dark hairs. The small premolar tooth is invisible from outside or even absent. Found in similar range and habitats to the Common Pipistrelle but especially in the mountains.

NOCTULE

Nyctalus noctula **7–8·5cm; wingspan max 40cm**

1*

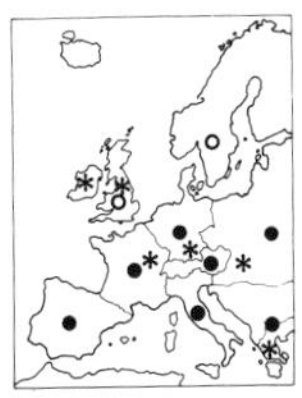

One of the large European bats. Fur dark reddish or yellowish-brown all over and face and ears dark. The tragus is wide and rounded.

Often flies by day, high in the sky, emitting an audible squeak. Night flight is zig-zag and lower, and the high-pitched call cannot be heard. Hibernates in large groups of hundreds or thousands in hollow trees.

Fairly common and widespread in most of Europe to 60°N, including Britain, especially in deciduous woodland, parkland, etc. in the lowlands.

Leisler's Bat (1): smaller, grey-brown fur, hairs darker at base. North of the Loire. The related Greater Noctule is the largest European bat, but only recorded in C. & SE. Europe.

SEROTINE

6–8cm; wingspan c. 35cm *Eptesicus serotinus*

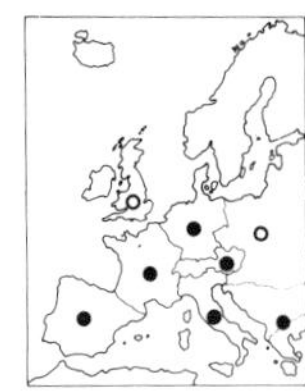

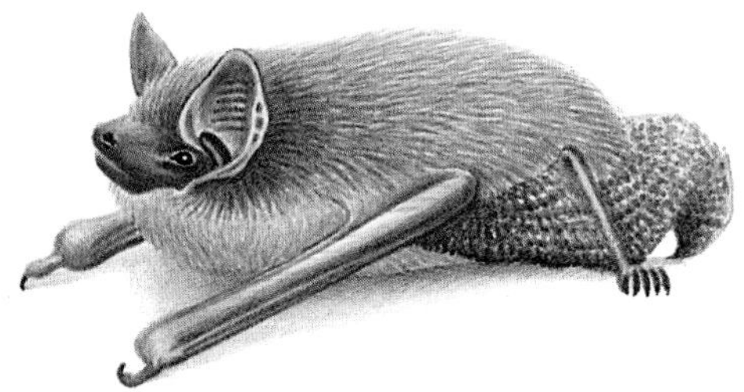

A fairly large bat, with a short portion of tail (approx. 6mm) projecting beyond the wing membrane. Fur greyish-brown. The ear has a short blunt tragus.

Slow fluttering flight alternating with rapid vertical dives. Flies at sunset or just after and catches insects in the air. Roosts in hollow trees and buildings.

It lives mainly in open woodland, copses, parkland, etc., throughout Europe north to SE. England and Denmark. It is sometimes seen in villages and towns.

Noctule (*N. noctula*) and *Myotis* bats do not have a projecting tail.

NORTHERN BAT

Eptesicus nilssoni **5–7cm; wingspan max. 27cm**

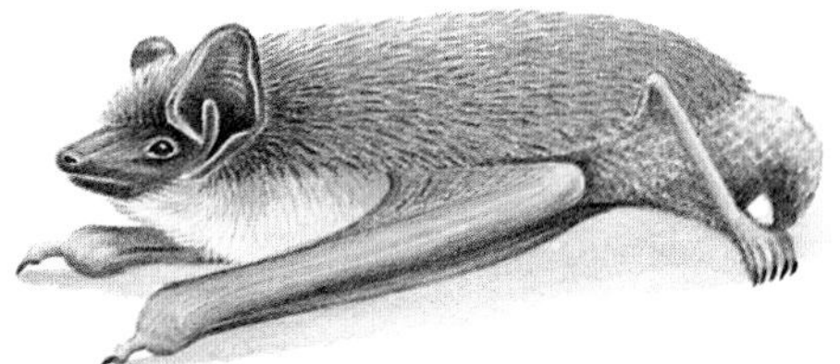

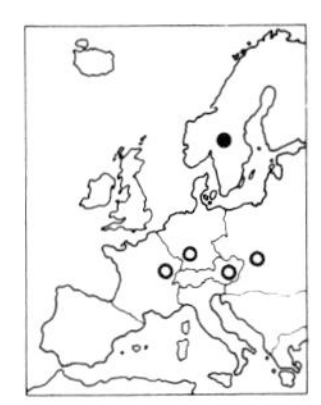

A smallish bat with shining, almost golden fur, the hair on back being dark with light tips. Underside paler. The tail projects slightly (2–3mm) beyond wing membrane. The face and ears are dark and the tragus broad and rounded.

Flies around dusk and again around dawn, catching insects in the air. Lives in a range of habitats, in woodland, farmland, villages and in mountains up to 2000m.

The most northerly of European bats. Locally common in parts of its range through central Europe into Scandinavia and west to the French Alps. Range extends into the Arctic Circle.

Considerably smaller than the **Serotine** (*E. serotinus*) and is distinguished by its colour from other small bats.

COMMON LONG-EARED BAT

4–5cm; wingspan c. 25cm *Plecotus auritus*

1*

A small bat with enormously long ears (3–3·8cm) meeting on top of the head. The tragus is transparent. Its fur is light greyish-brown on back, whitish underneath.

Feeds chiefly on moths and butterflies. It flies at dusk, slowly circling through trees and around buildings, sometimes taking insects from leaves. When hibernating, the folded wings hide the long ears and only the tragus is visible.

Lives in woodland, parkland and gardens over most of Europe including Britain, but not the far south or far north. It roosts and hibernates in attics, under tiles and in caves.

The **Grey Long-eared Bat (1)** has a less transparent tragus and grey fur without any brown. It is more southerly in range, reaching only SE. England.

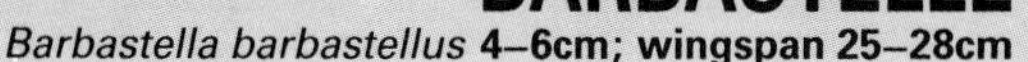

BARBASTELLE

Barbastella barbastellus **4–6cm; wingspan 25–28cm**

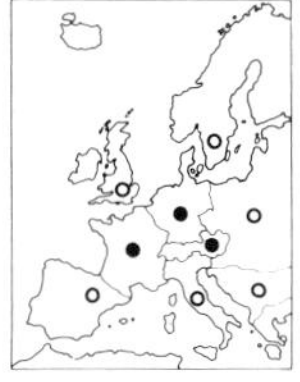

A smallish bat with short broad black ears meeting on the forehead and a small black face like a pug-dog. The fur on the back is dark with pale tips, giving it a frosted appearance.

Flies at sunset and before dawn; may produce a deep buzz and harsh squeaks. By day it roosts alone or in small colonies in holes in buildings, trees, walls. Feeds in flight on moths, flies and gnats. Hibernates in caves, mines and cellars.

Occurs throughout most of western and central Europe except far south, Ireland, Scotland and most of Scandinavia. In southern Europe it is found mostly in the hills.

None: ears and face are distinctive.

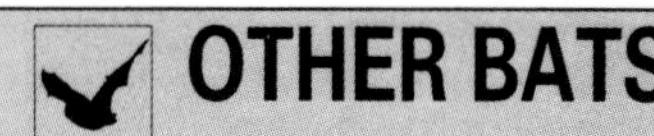

OTHER BATS

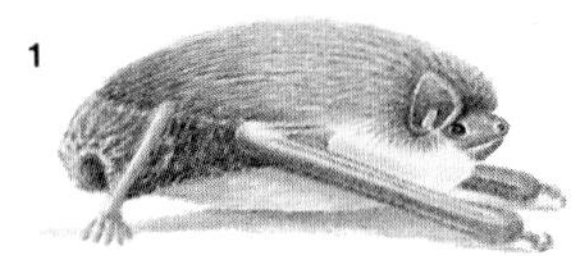

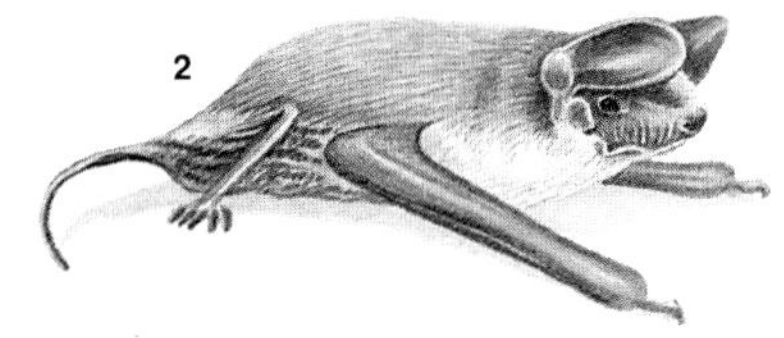

Schreiber's Bat (*Miniopterus schreibersi*) (**1**) is a medium-sized bat with long narrow wings and somewhat resembles a swift in flight. Occurs south from central France in rocky areas.

The very large **European Free-tailed Bat** (*Tadarida teniotis*) (**2**) (body length 8·2–8.7cm) has a long thick tail projecting from the wing membrane, and thick wrinkled lips. It lives in hills and mountains in the Mediterranean area, Spain and Italy. Often active in mild weather in winter.

The medium-sized **Particoloured Bat** (*Vespertilio murinus*) (**3**) has silvery tips to fur on back, giving it a frosted look, and white underside. Face and ears are dark. It remains active in winter even in cold weather. It occurs in central Europe west to eastern France and in southern Scandinavia.

BROWN BEAR

Ursus arctos

1·3–2·5m; tail 5–15cm

One of the largest European mammals, weighing up to 200kg. Coat thick and brown, varying from light brownish-grey to nearly black. Thick legs, a powerful neck and a hump at shoulders.

Mostly nocturnal. Omnivorous, eats grubs, insects, berries, roots and small mammals. Makes a den in a hollow tree or cave where it hibernates in winter. Leaves excavated anthills, overturned rocks and scratchmarks on trees and shrubs.

Coniferous forest from Scandinavia eastwards. A few individuals still survive in the Alps and Pyrenees.

None.

RED FOX

60–90cm; tail 35–45cm *Vulpes vulpes*

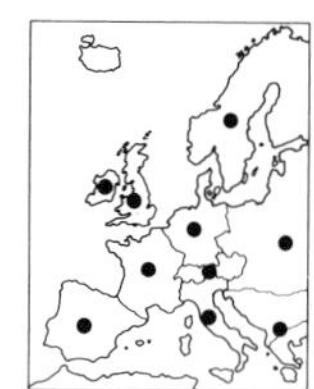

A common and familiar European animal, like a small to medium-sized dog and weighing 5–15kg. Coat bright red-brown, often mixed with black. Belly, chest and tip of bushy tail are white. It has a pointed nose and large ears.

Mainly nocturnal but often seen in daytime. Hunts small rodents, eats birds and their eggs, scavenges on refuse tips and in dustbins. Digs a den or lives in an old badger set. Strong-smelling urine and droppings mark its territory.

A highly adaptable animal, living in all types of countryside and in parks and waste ground in cities. Throughout Europe.

None: the colour, pointed nose and drooping bushy tail distinguish it from a domestic dog.

ARCTIC FOX

Alopex lagopus

50–85cm; tail 30–55cm

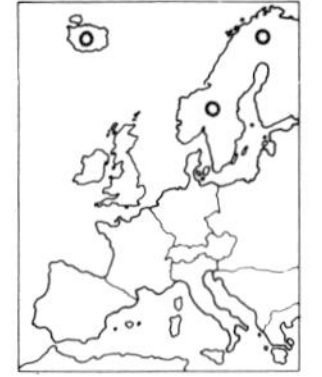

Exists in two colour forms. In one, the summer coat is brownish grey on face, back and outsides of legs, greyish white below, and in winter all white. The other (the Blue Fox) is blue-grey all the year round.

Active during the day, usually seen moving at a gallop. Preys chiefly on lemmings and other voles, but will eat birds, eggs, carrion and even berries when necessary. Lives in dens dug in sandy soil.

Lives in tundra and open mountain country with suitable soil for digging. Found in Iceland, mountains in Scandinavia and eastwards beyond the Arctic Circle.

None.

JACKAL

65–105cm; tail 20–40cm *Canis aureus*

A medium-sized animal between a fox and a large dog in size. Greyish coat on back shades into golden-brown on flanks and legs. It has large ears and relatively small paws.

Generally solitary and nocturnal, its presence revealed by a mournful howling. Omnivorous, eating berries and fruit, scavenging around farms and rubbish tips, and preying on birds and small mammals.

In Europe found in open terrain in Greece and neighbouring countries.

Wolf: larger, heavier in build. The Jackal is best distinguished from similar domestic dogs by its large ears and drooping tail, and its solitary and nocturnal habits.

WOLF

Canis lupus 90–150cm; tail 35–50cm

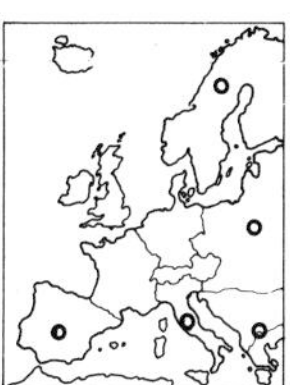

Large carnivorous animal weighing up to 80kg (male). Coat grey or yellowish-grey. Face broad with a thick ruff of hair behind cheeks. The bushy tail is carried drooping.

A social animal living and hunting in a family group or small pack except where numbers are very small. Mostly nocturnal, ranging over wide areas and preying mainly on deer. Howling may be heard day and night.

Now very rare in western Europe, populations of only a few hundred remaining in Spain, Portugal, Italy and Greece in remote areas and reserves. Main population in Russia eastwards.

Jackal: smaller, larger ears. The Wolf is distinguished from a large Alsatian or similar domestic dogs by the broader face, thick ruff of hair, drooping tail and head held low.

RACCOON-DOG

55–80cm; tail 15–25cm *Nyctereutes procyonoides*

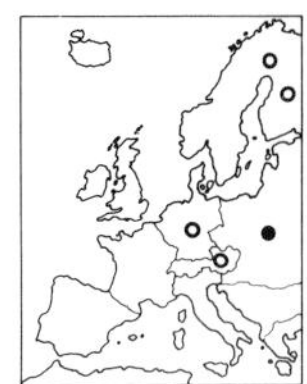

Medium-sized animal like a short-legged dog, with a thick brownish grey coat and a broad face with distinctive black mask. Ears short and rounded. Bushy tail is dark above and lighter beneath.

Nocturnal and solitary, preying on small rodents, fish, etc. Also eats insects and plant material. In the north goes into semi-hibernation in winter in a den.

Central Europe westwards through Germany and just into eastern France. Lives in woodland with thick undergrowth, especially near rivers and lakes. Introduced from Asia.

Raccoon.

RACCOON

Procyon lotor

50–70cm; tail 20–25cm

A medium-sized animal with a grey coat and distinctive black mask on face. Tail bushy and ringed with black.

Lives in woodland, especially oakwoods, near water. A good climber, often nesting high in a hollow tree. It is omnivorous, eating acorns, fruit, berries and grain as well as insects and grubs, birds' eggs and small mammals.

Introduced from North America and now found in Germany and neighbouring areas.

None.

WEASEL

17–38cm; tail 3–12cm *Mustela nivalis*

A small, slender animal, varying greatly in size from north (smaller) to south (larger). Reddish-brown coat with white underparts. No black tip to tail. Males larger than females. Some weasels turn white in the very far north.

Active day and night, hunting mainly small rodents, often underground in their runs. It is a good climber and takes young birds and eggs. Makes hissing, trilling and chirping noises.

Throughout Europe except Ireland, in all types of habitat.

Stoat: black tip to tail. Where the ranges overlap the stoat is generally the larger.

STOAT

Mustela erminea **18–30cm; tail 6–12cm**

Slender, long-bodied animal with a black-tipped tail. Coat reddish-brown on back with pale underparts. Coat turns pure white in north except for the black tail tip (and is then called ermine).

Hunts by night and day, preying on mice, voles, birds, etc. It is very active and inquisitive and will pop from its hiding place in a ditch or behind a log to watch a passer-by.

Throughout Europe except in the Mediterranean region, in a wide range of habitats. Requires very little cover.

Weasel: smaller (except in south) and no black tip to tail.

EUROPEAN MINK

35–40cm; tail 13–14cm *Mustela lutreola*

A long slender animal like a large weasel. Coat glossy dark brown all over except for white patch on upper lip and chin. Small ears and small webs on feet are adaptations to an aquatic life.

Lives beside water, in marshes and on the banks of rivers and lakes. Solitary and nocturnal, it is a good swimmer and diver, catching much of its food in the water. Feeds on fish, amphibians, small rodents, crayfish and other invertebrates.

In western Europe found only in a small area in western France, the main population being in eastern Europe.

Western Polecat; the **Otter** is much larger. **American Mink** escaped from fur farms are not generally found in the same range, and have white on the chin only.

AMERICAN MINK

Mustela vison

30–45cm; tail 15–20cm

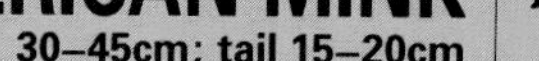

Very similar to the European Mink but has a patch of white on chin only and none on upper lip. Sometimes 'blue' or white mink recently escaped from fur farms may be seen, but they do not become established in the wild.

Mostly nocturnal. An expert swimmer, feeding on fish, amphibians and small mammals. Leaves piles of foul-smelling droppings prominently on rocks in river, etc. to mark its territory.

Beside water. Feral populations escaped from fur farms have become established in parts of Britain, Scandinavia and in isolated areas on continent.

Western Polecat; the **Otter** is much larger.

WESTERN POLECAT

30–45cm; tail 9–18cm (male) *Mustela putorius*

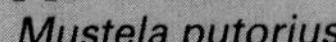

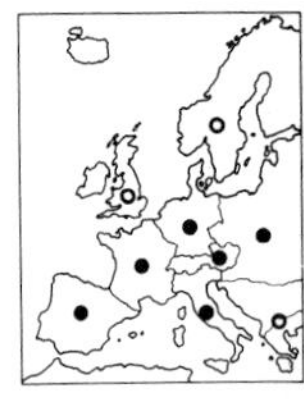

Long, slender, short-legged animal, dark brown all over except for white snout and patch behind eye. Lighter underfur shows through in places. Its relative the domesticated Ferret is very similar but generally lighter in colour.

Mainly nocturnal, preying on rodents, rabbits, frogs, and also takes invertebrates and carrion. Rarely climbs or swims. Releases a fetid scent when alarmed. Often found close to buildings.

Lives in lowland woods, also in marshes and on riverbanks. Throughout Europe except Ireland and northern Scandinavia. In Britain only in Wales and borders.

Mink: uniformly dark brown, usually seen in water; **Martens**: larger, yellow or white patch on throat and chest.

PINE MARTEN

Martes martes

35–55cm; tail 17–28cm

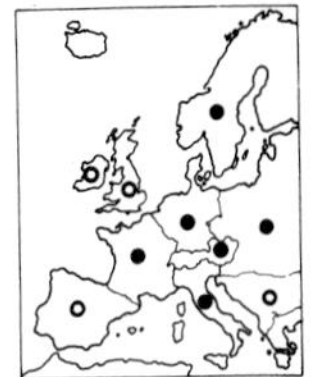

A medium-sized animal, long and slender with a fairly bushy tail. Rich brown coat with an irregular yellowish-white patch on throat and chest. Ears prominent and paler than rest of body.

Solitary and mainly nocturnal, may be seen at dawn and dusk. Excellent climber. Preys mainly on rodents, including voles and mice. Den is made in a hollow tree or crack in rocks.

Coniferous and mixed deciduous forest, throughout Europe to northern Spain. Not in Greece. In Britain only in Scotland and locally in northern England and north Wales.

Beech Marten; Western Polecat.

BEECH MARTEN

40–48cm; tail 22–26cm *Martes foina*

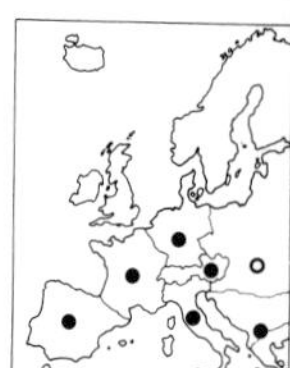

Very similar to the Pine Marten but throat patch pure white, sometimes extending down front legs a short way.

Much more common around buildings and even in built-up areas than the Pine Marten. Solitary and mainly nocturnal, taking mice, shrews and birds. An excellent climber. Sometimes nests in buildings.

In deciduous woodland and rocky hillsides, and also increasingly in built-up areas. Throughout southern and central Europe eastwards. Not in Britain or Scandinavia.

Pine Marten; **Western Polecat.**

OTTER

Lutra lutra

55–100cm; tail 30–55cm

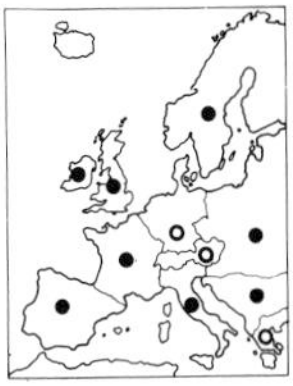

Long-bodied and short-legged, with a long tail tapering from a thick base. Feet webbed, and is an agile, powerful and rapid swimmer. Dense dark brown fur with a paler throat. Conspicuous whiskers and small ears.

Solitary, elusive, mainly nocturnal. Catches fish of various sorts, and small mammals, amphibians and crustaceans. Makes a den among tree roots or under rocks on the river bank. Droppings deposited prominently on rocks mark its territory.

Lives beside seashores, rivers and lakes. Throughout Europe, but has become rare and has disappeared entirely from many areas.

Coypu and **Beaver**: plumper, less rapid and agile swimmers, easily distinguished out of the water. **Mink**: smaller.

BADGER

70–90cm; tail 12–20cm *Meles meles*

A heavily-built animal weighing up to 17kg. The black and white striped face, black undersides and shaggy grey back make it easy to identify.

A social animal living in small groups. It is nocturnal, coming out to feed after dusk. Eats earthworms, insects, birds, eggs and small mammals. Excavates extensive tunnels leading to a set, with mounds of earth outside entrances.

Likes deciduous woodland in cultivated areas. Throughout Europe except in far north and some Mediterranean islands.

None.

WOLVERINE

Gulo gulo

70–80cm; tail 15–25cm

A dark brown, heavy-looking animal like a small bear, but with a bushy tail and a broad light brown stripe along each brow and side. It weighs up to 25kg, the female being slightly smaller than the male.

A solitary hunter, wandering over large areas and killing deer and smaller mammals. Also takes carrion. Den is made among rocks or in a thicket. Prey is broken up and hidden. Young born in early spring in a den deep in the snow.

Found in the mountains and tundra of Scandinavia eastwards.

None.

GENET

47–60cm; tail 40–50cm *Genetta genetta*

A slim, short-legged carnivore with a spotted coat and a very long tail ringed with dark and light bands. Ears prominent and muzzle pointed.

Solitary and nocturnal, hunting mainly small rodents, birds and reptiles. It also eats berries and fruit. An expert climber.

In Europe only in Spain and southeastern France, and the Balearic Islands. Lives in woodland and scrub, up to 2000m in the Pyrenees.

None.

ICHNEUMON OR EGYPTIAN MONGOOSE

Herpestes ichneumon **50–55cm; tail 35–45cm**

Slim, short-legged carnivore with a coarse, grizzled brown and grey coat and a long tapering tail. Pale tip to tail.

Mainly nocturnal but also sometimes active by day. Solitary, except for a female with young. It hunts rabbits, rodents, birds, snakes and other reptiles.

An African and Near Eastern species which has been introduced at some time into southern Spain and Portugal. Lives on scrubby rocky hillsides.

Polecat; **Martens**.

WILD CAT

50–65cm; tail 30cm *Felis silvestris*

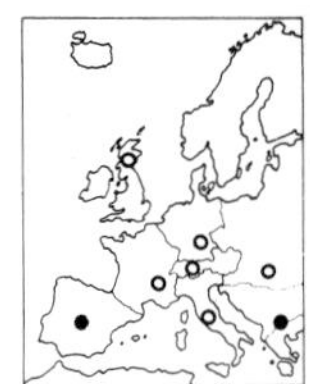

The size of a large domestic cat, the Wild Cat resembles a large and very fierce tabby. The coat is always striped, never blotched, and the thick, blunt-ended tail is ringed with black. It can interbreed with the domestic cat.

Mainly solitary and nocturnal. An agile hunter, stalking its prey on the ground. Eats rodents, rabbits and other small mammals, sometimes fish. Mews and purrs like a domestic cat, but unlike a domestic cat it does not bury its droppings.

Iberia, southern Italy, the Balkan Peninsula, and also in Scotland and mountains in central Europe. It lives in forest and scrubland in the south.

Feral domestic tabby cats can be distinguished by their thinner and more pointed tails, and are often patterned with blotches as well as, or instead of, stripes.

PARDEL LYNX

Lynx pardina

80–110cm; tail 12cm

A large, long-legged cat with yellow brown coat spotted with black and a black tip to the short tail. Tufted ears and cheeks, often with a pronounced black stripe from eye to cheek.

Solitary and nocturnal, hunting hares, rodents and other small mammals and birds. Makes a den amongst rocks or in a hollow tree.

The form of lynx found in the Iberian Peninsula, where it lives in thick scrub in some lowlands, and in the mountains of central and southern Spain and Portugal.

None.

LYNX

80–130cm; tail 15–20cm *Lynx lynx*

A large cat, with long legs, tufted ears and cheeks, and variable darker spotting to coat, usually spotted at least on flanks and tops of legs. Colour varies from yellow brown to pale yellow grey. Short tail has a black tip.

Solitary and nocturnal, hunting on the ground or waiting for its prey crouched in a tree. Makes a den amongst rocks or in a hollow tree. Hunts mainly hares, rodents, deer and ground birds. Male makes a wailing call in spring.

Main area of distribution is the northern coniferous forest from central Scandinavia eastwards. Isolated populations survive in the Alps, Carpathians and Balkans.

None.

RED SQUIRREL

Sciurus vulgaris **20–28cm; tail 15–24cm**

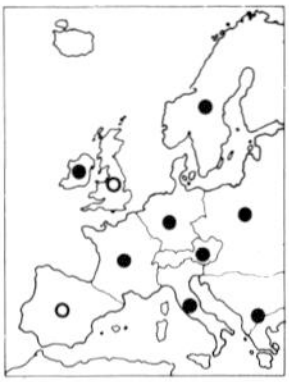

Bushy tail, warm reddish-brown to greyish-brown back and sides with paler underparts, and chattering call make this animal easy to identify as it scampers along a branch. All-black individuals sometimes occur. Prominent ear tufts.

A tree-dweller, active throughout the day, sometimes coming down to the ground to gather fallen nuts, fungi, beechmast, etc. which it stores. Makes a domed nest in the fork of a tree. Discards cones with scales chewed off completely.

The common squirrel of continental Europe, found in most wooded regions, parks and gardens. Has disappeared from much of Britain since the introduction of the Grey Squirrel.

Grey Squirrel (Britain only). Siberian Chipmunks escaped from captivity (France, Germany, Holland, Austria) have five dark stripes along the back and a less bushy tail.

GREY SQURREL

25–30cm; tail 20–25cm *Sciurus carolinensis*

A North American introduction, larger than the Red Squirrel and always grey or greyish-brown, with often a white fringe to tail. No ear tufts.

Lives and nests in trees but spends part of its time feeding on the ground. Eats nuts, acorns, beechmast, green plants, fungi and roots.

Common in parks, gardens, deciduous and mixed woodland in England and Wales, where it has replaced the Red Squirrel. Not found in continental Europe.

Red Squirrel (in E. Ireland, southern Scotland, Norfolk, Wales); smaller, conspicuous ear tufts, and usually much more reddish-brown.

EUROPEAN SOUSLIK

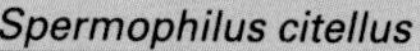

Spermophilus citellus **20–22cm; tail 6–7cm**

A ground squirrel, about the size of a guinea pig, often sitting up on its hind legs. Light yellow-grey coat, furry tail and small inconspicuous ears.

Lives in underground burrows, often in large colonies. Active by day, giving a sharp whistle when alarmed. Eats grass seeds and grain which it carries in cheek pouches. Hibernates below ground in winter, emerging with new-born young in spring.

Dry grasslands and cultivated land in Southeastern Europe, ranging west into parts of Czechoslovakia, Poland and Eastern Germany.

Spotted Souslik: distinctly spotted coat. **Common Hamster**: fatter, short tail, multicoloured coat with dark underparts, and larger ears.

ALPINE MARMOT

50–55cm; tail 15cm *Marmota marmota*

A large, heavily built ground squirrel, the size of a small dog, with a large head and short legs. Often sits upright. Dense greyish coat and furry tail.

Active by day, feeding on grasses and other green plants. Lives in colonies in deep burrows in soil or scree in which it hibernates in winter. Gives a sharp whistling alarm signal when disturbed.

High open pastures in the Alps and Tatra mountains of Czechoslovakia. Introduced into the Pyrenees.

None.

FLYING SQUIRREL 

Pteromys volans **14–20cm; tail 9–14cm**

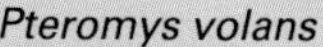

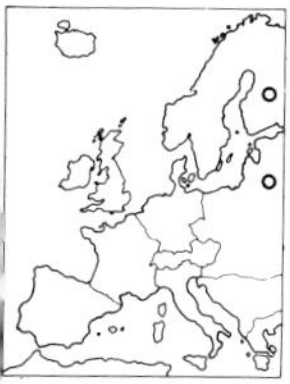

A small squirrel with light grey fur on back and sides and white underparts. A broad fold of skin along the side of body from front to hind leg is extended to support the animal as it glides from branch to branch. The eyes are large.

A shy, nocturnal animal. Nests and stores food in hollow trees. Feeds on alder and birch catkins and small twigs, and all sorts of other plant food. Also takes birds' eggs.

Mixed forest from Finland eastwards.

None.

FAT DORMOUSE

15–20cm; tail 11–15cm *Glis glis*

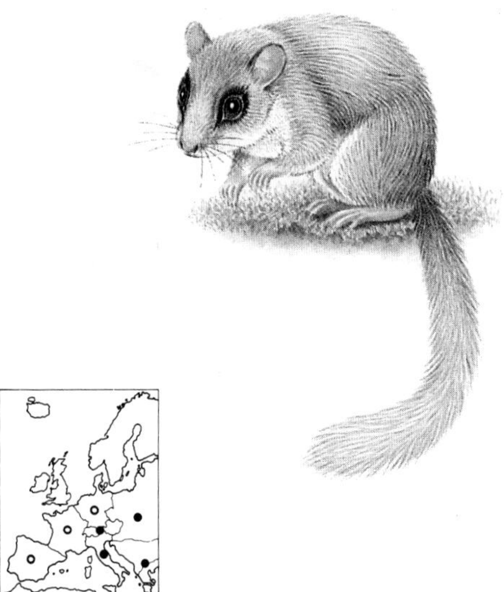

A large grey dormouse with a bushy tail and white underparts. The large eyes appear even bigger due to the black rings around them. Long whiskers. Excellent climber with feet adapted for gripping.

Nocturnal, coming out after dusk to feed on nuts, berries, fruit, seeds and bark, and also possibly small birds. It makes various noises including a harsh creaking sound. Hibernates in hollows below ground lined with dry grass, etc.

Deciduous and mixed woodland, coming into parks and orchards. Throughout central and southern Europe except most of Spain. In Britain very local in southeast England.

Grey Squirrel: larger and active in daytime.

HAZEL DORMOUSE

Muscardinus avellanarius **6–9cm; tail 6–8cm**

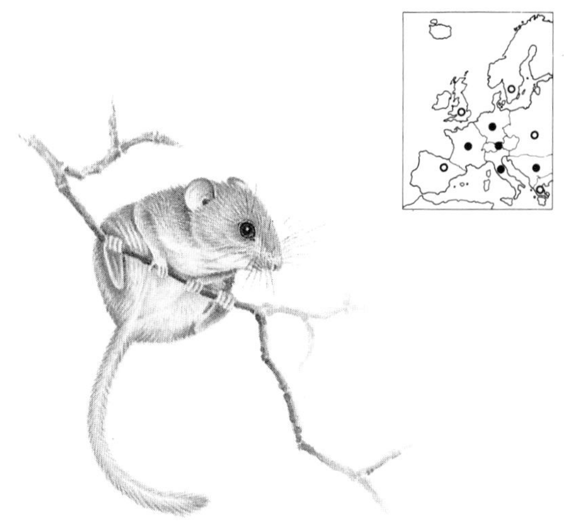

Small golden-brown to fox-red dormouse with white underparts, large eyes, small ears and a long bushy tail which is fluffed out when angry or frightened.

Nocturnal. An excellent climber spending most of its time in trees and bushes. Eats hazelnuts, other nuts, juniper and rowan berries and buds and shoots. Makes a round nest with a side entrance in a thick bush. Hibernates in winter.

A range of habitats, including hazel copses, forest edges, swampy forest, parks and gardens. Throughout most of Europe except Iberia, reaching southern Britain and Scandinavia.

Garden Dormouse; dormice can be distinguished from other small nocturnal rodents by their bushy tails.

GARDEN DORMOUSE

10–17cm; tail 9–12cm *Eliomys quercinus*

A distinctively coloured dormouse with black eye stripes and black down outside of front legs. Tail has a flattened tufted black and white tip. Ears large.

Nocturnal and an agile climber, but often found on ground. Makes a nest in a hole in a tree or crevice in wall. Eats a variety of food including nuts and fruit and also insects, snails, eggs, etc. Hibernates from October to April.

Woodland, gardens and orchards, throughout western and central Europe except Britain, Holland, northern Germany and Scandinavia.

Fat Dormouse.

NORWAY LEMMING

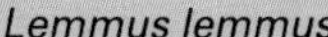
Lemmus lemmus **13–15cm; tail 15–19mm**

A small, blunt-snouted animal with a short tail and soft, boldly coloured black, yellow and yellowish-brown coat. It is easy to identify, especially in years when its numbers reach almost plague proportions and large migrations occur.

Lives in uplands, feeding on mosses, grasses, sedges and other plants. Makes shallow summer burrows, and tunnels and winter nests under the snow. It is often noisy, hissing and squeaking loudly.

The mountains of Norway and Sweden.

Wood Lemming: smaller, slate grey coat. Other voles found in the same regions are also smaller and reddish-brown to grey in colour.

WOOD LEMMING

8–11cm; tail 1–1·5cm *Myopus schisticolor*

A small shy rodent, more common in some years than others. Fur soft and dark grey with a rusty brown patch on lower back in adults. Tail short and inconspicuous.

Makes burrows, nests and runways in moss in damp coniferous forest. Feeds mainly on moss and takes some other plant food.

Southeastern Norway through Scandinavia eastwards.

The short tail and dark grey colour distinguish it from other voles of the same size living in this region.

GREY-SIDED VOLE

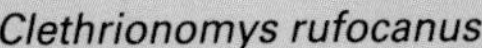

Clethrionomys rufocanus **11–13cm; tail 2·5–4cm**

A small rodent with soft fur, grey on sides and underparts, with a narrow band of reddish fur along the middle of the back.

Active during day and night. A good climber, feeding on shoots, buds, leaves and bark. Makes runways in grass and moss.

Found in the mountains of Scandinavia eastwards, on high moors and in the alpine birch forest.

Bank Vole: smaller, red fur on back extending further down sides and a noticeably longer tail. **Northern Red-backed Vole**: only in far north, light yellowish-brown on sides.

BANK VOLE

8–13cm; tail 3·5–7cm *Clethrionomys glareolus*

Small, round-bodied, reddish-brown rodent with a relatively long tail. The russet back merges into the greyer fur of sides and the distinctly lighter underparts. Tail darker above, light below. Eyes and ears larger than other voles.

Active day and night and throughout the winter. It makes runways in grass and underground but also climbs above ground. Feeds on buds and leaves as well as insects and other small invertebrates. Nests under fallen logs and tree roots.

Common throughout Europe except Iberia, parts of Ireland and the borders of the Adriatic. Found in woods of all kinds and dense shrubby undergrowth.

Shrews: generally smaller, snout long and pointed. **Mice**: tail longer and bare, prominent ears. Other **voles**.

NORTHERN & SOUTHERN WATER VOLES

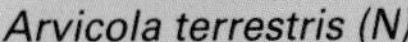

Arvicola terrestris (N) **12–23cm; tail 5–14cm**

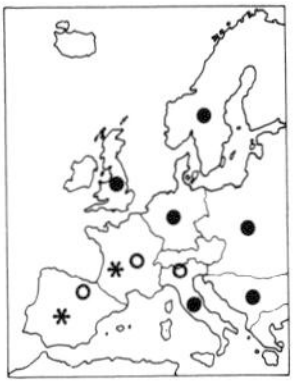

The largest native European voles. Fur dark, sometimes almost black, with paler underparts. Long tail, ears small and covered with fur. Hindfeet much larger than the front feet.

They are expert swimmers and are generally found beside water, although *A. terrestris* also lives in drier places. Make burrows in the river banks. Feed on plants, especially sedges and rushes. *A. terrestris* stores roots for the winter.

A. terrestris (illustrated) is common throughout Europe westwards to E. France, and in UK and Pyrenees. It is replaced in W. France and Iberia by the outwardly identical *A. sapidus*.*

Where the species overlap *A. sapidus* is always the larger, with tail length up to 14cm. **Water Shrews**: long pointed snouts, black velvety fur on back and white underparts.

COMMON PINE VOLE

8–10cm; tail 2·5–4cm *Pitymys subterraneus*

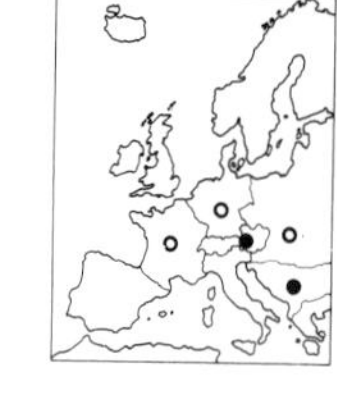

A small short-tailed vole with short thick yellowish-brown fur, darker on back. Eyes small, and small ears almost hidden by fur. All pine voles have five pads on the soles of their hindfeet compared with six in *Microtus* species.

Active mainly at night. It lives underground much of the time in extensive burrows just under the surface. Feeds on roots, bulbs, etc. gathered underground.

Found in meadowland, open grassland and open woodland where soil is suitable for burrowing. Northern and central France eastwards into central Europe and up to 2000m in Alps.

Alpine Pine Vole: only in Alps, outwardly indistinguishable. Savi's Pine Vole: W. France & Italy, lighter in colour, last upper molar has only three cusps; **Mediterranean Pine Vole**.

COMMON VOLE

Microtus arvalis **9–12cm; tail 3–4·5cm**

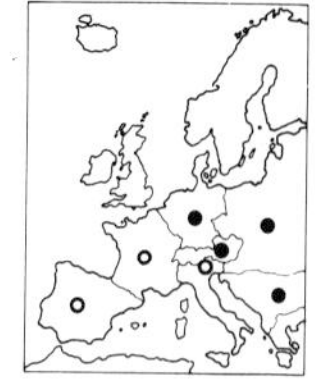

Fur short and neat, greyish brown on back, paler undersides. Ears almost hairless inside with a thick fringe of hairs around top edge.

Active day and night. Excavates underground tunnels in which it lives. Eats grasses and other green plants, and bark in winter.

Common in dryish meadowland where it likes to live in the shorter grass. Throughout most of Europe except UK, Scandinavia and around Mediterranean.

Field Vole: shaggier, more unkempt appearance, small extra lobe on inside of middle upper cheek tooth. **Root Vole**: an E. European species, only found in Netherlands in W Europe.

FIELD VOLE

8–13cm; tail 2–4·5cm *Microtus agrestis*

Fur dark brownish-grey on back with sides paler, often looking rather shaggy at close quarters. Middle upper cheek tooth has a small extra lobe on inside.

Active day and night. Makes runways in long grass and also feeds mainly on grasses, supplemented by bark in winter. Has a low chirping call and will come quite close to a patient observer.

Common in varied habitats throughout Europe except south and Ireland. Especially likes damp ground and long grass. Less common than Common Vole in grazed areas.

Common Vole: neater coat, rarely found in damp areas, otherwise difficult to tell apart except by teeth. **Root Vole**: only in Netherlands in W. Europe, tail proportionately longer.

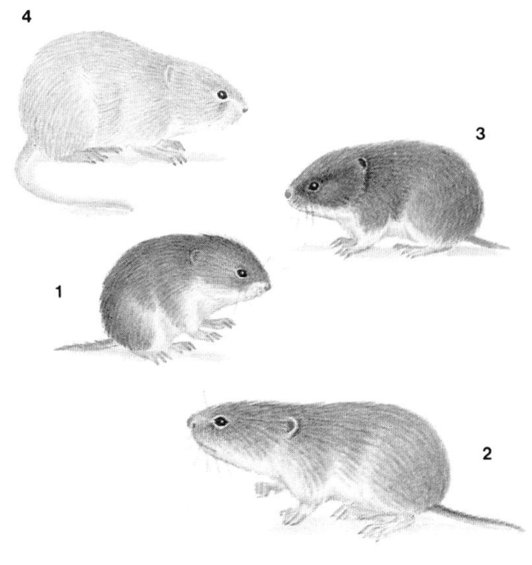

Northern Red-backed Vole (*Clethrionomys rutilus*) (**1**). A medium-sized vole, light bright reddish brown, paler below, with a short well-haired tail with a terminal tuft. Replaces the Bank Vole in northern Scandinavia, living in birch woodland and willow copses.

Root Vole (*Microtus oeconomus*) (**2**). Very similar to Field Vole but darker, and tail slightly longer. Eastern Europe to Norway, in damp grasslands and swamps.

Mediterranean Pine Vole (*Pitymys duodecimcostatus*) (**3**). Very soft dense yellowish brown fur above and silvery grey below. In Med. regions of Spain and France, in grassland.

Snow Vole (*Microtus nivalis*) (**4**). Largish vole, pale greyish brown, tail long and very light. Prominent whiskers. Scattered throughout Alps and mountains in Spain & SE. Europe. Lives on open mountain slopes, likes to bask on rocks in sunshine. Also in low wooded hills in S. France.

COMMON HAMSTER

18–30cm; tail 3–7cm *Cricetus cricetus*

Black undersides and variegated golden-brown coat distinguish this small animal, whose smaller relative the Golden Hamster is a familiar pet.

A burrowing animal, living in extensive underground tunnels. Feeds on many kinds of wild and crop plants, carrying food in its cheek pouches. Hibernates underground when temperature falls below 10 °C. Hisses and squeaks when annoyed.

An animal of the steppe grasslands, it ranges westwards in isolated populations as far as eastern France.

None.

LESSER MOLE-RAT

Spalax leucodon **15–24cm; no tail**

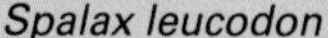

A rodent well adapted for an underground life. It lacks external ears and tail, and eyes are overgrown with skin. Powerful front teeth are used for digging. The head merges into body without a perceptible neck. Coat yellow-brown.

Lives almost permanently underground in extensive tunnels excavated with the aid of the powerful front teeth. Active mainly at night. Eats roots, bulbs, etc.

Grassland and cultivated land in Greece and the Balkan peninsula.

The slightly larger Greater Mole-rat occurs further east. Otherwise none.

HARVEST MOUSE

6–7·5cm; tail 5–7cm *Micromys minutus*

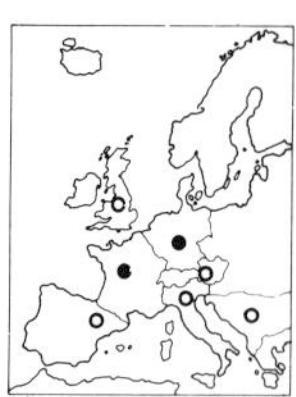

The smallest European mouse, weighing up to 11g. Small ears and rich russet brown coat with white underparts. Tail very long and prehensile.

An expert climber, running up grass and cornstalks and gripping with its long tail. It builds a round nest of grass in stems of grass and shrubs about half a metre above ground. Eats mainly seeds and green plants, and in winter, insects.

Throughout central and western Europe, except north and south, living in dense vegetation and cultivated land. Formerly common in cornfields.

Shrews and **voles**: shorter hairier tails, velvety fur and inconspicuous or hidden ears.

YELLOW-NECKED MOUSE

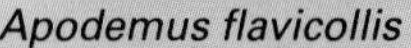

Apodemus flavicollis **9–13cm; tail 9–13cm**

Coat brownish grey to golden brown on back and sides, pale underparts. The yellowish-brown patch under the neck between the front legs is often not present in the south. Tail has many closely spaced rings.

Lives mostly in woods. Mainly vegetarian, eating seeds, nuts, and shoots, but also takes small invertebrates. Leaves nutshells opened with a hole, with an edging of tooth marks around the outside of the rim. Makes burrows in soft soil.

Central Europe west to eastern France and southeastern England. Up to 2000m in the Alps.

Wood Mouse: smaller and duller in colour. **Shrews**: much smaller, long pointed snouts; **Voles**: less conspicuous ears and blunter snouts.

WOOD MOUSE

8–10cm; tail 7–9cm *Apodemus sylvaticus*

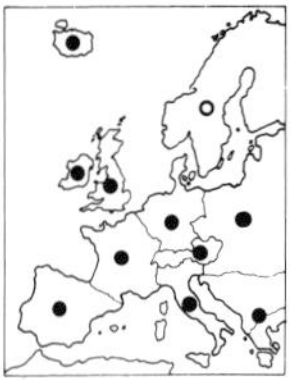

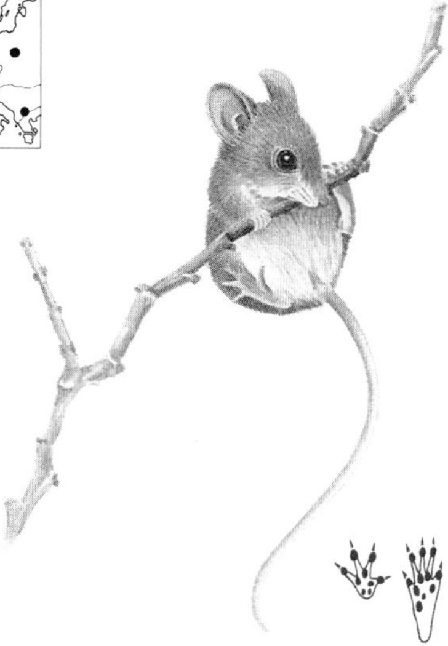

A small mouse with large ears and eyes, lacking the yellow patch on chest.

Nocturnal. Eats seeds, nuts, plants and earthworms. Very agile and skilled climber. Digs burrows in soft soil. Leaves nutshells opened by a hole, with toothmarks round rim.

Common throughout Europe, except central and northern Scandinavia. Found in many places, often coming into gardens.

Yellow-necked Mouse; **House Mouse**; **Shrews**: smaller, long pointed snouts; **Voles**: inconspicuous ears and blunter snouts.

STRIPED FIELD MOUSE

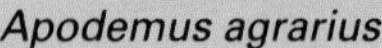

Apodemus agrarius **7–12cm; tail 6·5–9cm**

Distinctive black stripe down back to base of tail. Coat yellow or russet brown with paler underparts. Tail shorter than head and body.

Active during the day. It lives in a range of habitats, especially in damp places. Eats seeds, insects and their larvae, worms, snails and even small vertebrates if already dead.

An eastern European species, ranging westwards into northern Germany and Denmark and into northern Italy.

Birch Mice: nocturnal, longer tails.

SOUTHERN & NORTHERN BIRCH MICE

5·5–7cm; tail 7–8·5cm *Sicista betulina (N)*

1

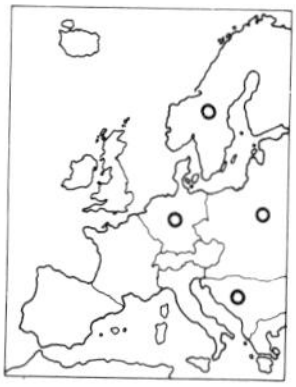

Small mouse-like rodents with tail more than 1½ times the length of the body. Black stripe from crown of head to base of tail is bordered by lighter hair than rest of coat in the Southern Birch Mouse, *S. subtilis* (**1**).

Rare and nocturnal, feeding mainly on insects but also seeds and fruit. Excellent climber, with paws adapted for gripping and climbing. Hibernates in hollow trees or below ground.

Birchwoods in Denmark, Scandinavia, Austria (*S. betulina*), the main range being to the east. *S. subtilis* is found in the north of the Balkan peninsula eastwards.

Striped Field Mouse: larger, shorter tail.

HOUSE MOUSE

Mus musculus **7–12cm; tail 5·5–9cm**

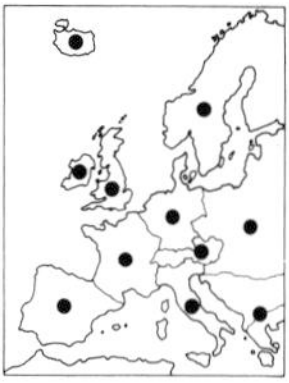

Very variable in coat colour and size, ranging from a yellowish-grey (in south) to dark grey-brown (in north). Tail quite thick and prominently ringed. Small notch on rear edge of front incisor teeth.

Where the House Mouse lives in association with man it is omnivorous and can become a pest. In the countryside it eats grain, small insects and other invertebrates. Often lives in houses where it makes nests under floors, etc.

Found throughout Europe. In northern and western Europe lives in close association with man, but around the Mediterranean inhabits open cultivated land.

Wood Mouse; **Yellow-necked Mouse**.

BLACK OR SHIP RAT

10–24cm; tail 11–26cm *Rattus rattus*

An agile rat with large hairless ears. Coat slate-grey, ears and paws pink and hairless. The long tail is scaly and pink throughout.

In towns and cities it lives in old houses, warehouses and other old buildings. Eats mainly vegetable food, especially fruit. It is now much less common than the Brown Rat.

Originally reached Europe along the trade routes and is found in cities and seaports around western Europe, and also in the countryside in southern Europe.

Brown Rat.

COMMON OR BROWN RAT

Rattus norvegicus **15–28cm; tail 9–23cm**

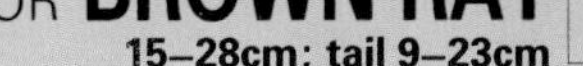

A medium-sized rodent with brown fur. Tail grey-brown above and paler below, and shorter than body.

Lives in close association with man and can become a serious pest and carrier of disease. Lives in sewers, warehouses, barns and refuse tips, as well as in the countryside.

Throughout western and central Europe except around the Mediterranean.

Black Rat: more lightly built and agile, coat slate-grey, less common.

MUSKRAT

24–40cm; tail 19–28cm *Ondatra zibethicus*

A medium-sized rodent, with very soft dense brown fur (musquash) and a long scaly tail flattened vertically. The large hindfeet are not webbed. Small inconspicuous ears.

Active in early morning, it is a powerful swimmer and diver. Makes burrows in river banks, and on still waters sometimes builds a domed nest of grasses and reeds up to a metre high. Eats all sorts of plants and small clams, mussels, etc.

Introduced from N. America for its fur, it now lives along coasts, lakes, rivers and streams throughout most of France, Germany and Central Europe.

Coypu: larger, tail round in cross-section and hindfeet webbed.
Beaver: much larger, tail flat and paddle-shaped.

COYPU OR NUTRIA

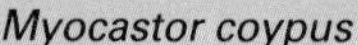

Myocastor coypus **36–65cm; tail 22–45cm**

A large rodent weighing up to 8kg, with a large head, orange front teeth and a long, scaly tail, round in cross-section and only sparsely haired. Webbed hindfeet. Dense fine brown underfur (nutria) with a longer coarser top coat.

Lives and breeds in tunnels in banks besides lakes, slow-flowing rivers and streams. A good swimmer and diver, it spends much time in the water, feeding on water plants.

Introduced from S. America for its fur and cannot survive very cold winters. Long-established populations in SE. England and parts of France, and elsewhere in Europe.

Muskrat: smaller, tail flattened sideways. **European Beaver**: much larger, tail flat and broad.

EUROPEAN BEAVER

70–100cm; tail 30–40cm *Castor fiber*

A very large rodent weighing up to 35kg, with thick brown fur almost concealing the small ears. The black, scaly, paddle-shaped tail is unique. Large hindfeet are webbed. Obvious orange-red front teeth and small eyes.

Mostly nocturnal, eating bark, twigs and many other types of plant food. Fells tres with its sharp teeth to build dams and lodges, houses of mud-caulked logs and twigs up to 2m high, where the beavers live on stored food in winter.

Beside lakes and slow-running rivers in deciduous or mixed forest. Sporadic in W. & C. Europe and Scandinavia. Indigenous to the Rhone delta, reintroduced elsewhere in France.

It is very much larger than the **Coypu** or **Muskrat** and is the only European rodent that fells trees, leaving the typically shaped stumps.

PORCUPINE

Hystrix cristata

50–70cm; tail 5–12cm

A large, slow-moving rodent, weighing up to 17kg, with long and short, black and white spines on back and tail. Stiff white hairs on crown and nape of neck are erected to form a crest when alarmed.

Nocturnal. Lives in deep burrows and caves. Makes a rattling noise with spines on tail when threatened. Feeds on green plants, fruit, roots and bark, holding food between the front paws.

S. & W. Italy and Sicily, in dry scrubland and cultivated land. Possibly introduced from Africa in Roman times.

None.

BROWN HARE

55–70cm; tail 7–12cm *Lepus europaeus*

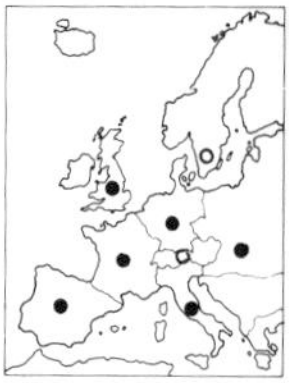

Larger than a rabbit, with long powerful hind legs and long ears tipped with black. Its yellowish-brown coat remains the same colour all the year round. The tail is black above and white underneath.

Mainly nocturnal, spending the day in a depression ('form') made in the grass. Eats all sorts of grasses, roots, buds and bark. The leaping gait is distinctive and in spring hares are often very active.

Open pastures, cultivated land and bushy scrub are favourite habitats. Throughout Europe except Ireland, Iberian peninsula and most of Scandinavia.

Cape Hare (*L. capensis*) (Iber.): smaller, fur of breast and flanks reddish-brown. **Mountain Hare:** smaller, tail all white. **Rabbit**: smaller, shorter legs, ears not black-tipped.

MOUNTAIN HARE

Lepus timidus

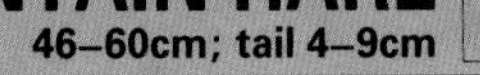

46–60cm; tail 4–9cm

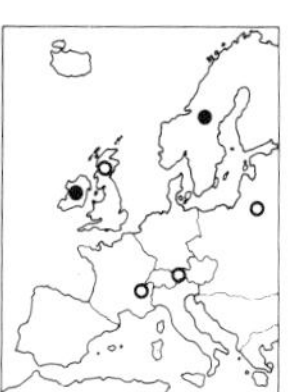

Summer coat grey-brown, white underparts; winter coat white (in north) or grey, while tips of ears remain black. Coat remains brown all year round in Ireland. Tail all white.

In winter often detected by its tracks in the snow. Unlike the Brown Hare it sometimes makes short burrows and occasionally gathers in large groups. It eats young twigs, bark, heather, bilberry plants etc.

Lives in open deciduous woodland and high moors. Found in Ireland, Scotland, and Scandinavia eastwards, but only in the Alps further south.

Brown Hare: larger, tail black above. **Rabbit**: generally not found in the same habitat. The Mountain Hare can interbreed with the Brown Hare where their ranges overlap.

RABBIT

35–50cm; tail 4–8cm *Oryctolagus cuniculus*

A burrowing animal with long ears, greyish-brown to black fur, paler undersides, and a white tail which is held up as a warning signal as the animal scampers away.

Active mainly at night but often seen in evening or early morning. Lives in large colonies in extensive burrows (warrens) in sandy or loamy soil. Eats all sorts of plant food and can be a serious pest of crops and plantations.

Common in cultivated land, dunes, edges of woodlands etc. except where subject to myxomatosis. Throughout Europe to Poland, except S. Italy and Sardinia.

Brown Hare and **Mountain Hare**: longer legs, black tips to the longer ears.

ROE DEER

Capreolus capreolus **95–135cm; tail 2–3cm**

A small deer standing up to 75cm at shoulder. Tail concealed in the white rump. Uniformly greyish to reddish brown, the male having white patches under throat and small antlers with knobbly bases and up to three points. Young have white spots.

Active day and night, but comes out to graze mainly at dusk and dawn. Congregates in large herds in winter. Eats mainly grass and herbs. The rut is in July and August when males compete for females. Alarm call is a repeated short bark.

Throughout most of Europe and locally abundant. Original habitat is forest but the Roe Deer is very adaptable and is increasingly coming into cultivated land.

Sika Deer and **Fallow Deer**: larger, spotted; **Muntjac** and **Chinese Water Deer**: no antlers, heavier bodied though often smaller, very restricted distribution.

FALLOW DEER

1·3–1·6m; tail 16–19cm *Cervus dama*

A medium-sized deer standing up to 1·1m high at shoulder. Mid to dark brown with white-spotted coat in summer, duller in winter. White patch bordered with black on rump, and black stripe down tail. Males bear antlers with wide flat blades.

Lives in herds, active during the day and night. Mainly grazes on grass, but also eats leaves and shoots of young trees. Often kept in parks. In late autumn males compete to gather a harem of females for mating.

Deciduous and mixed woodland, especially where interspersed with open spaces. Is patchily distributed throughout Europe, relatively common in southeastern England and central Europe.

Red Deer: larger, not spotted; **Sika Deer**: smaller, antlers not flattened.

RED DEER

Cervus elaphus **1·65–2·6m; tail 12–15cm**

A large deer standing up to 1·5m at shoulder. Coat reddish brown to grey brown. Males bear large, much-branched antlers and a mane of long hair on neck. Buff to yellowish rump patch with no black edge or stripe on tail. Young have white spots.

In woodland comes out mainly at night to graze, but in open country large herds are often seen during the day. The rut occurs during September when the roaring of the stags is commonly heard. Increasingly being farmed for venison.

Found in varied habitats from open deciduous forest to moorland. Throughout central and parts of western Europe, Scotland, and southern Scandinavia.

Fallow Deer; **Sika Deer**.

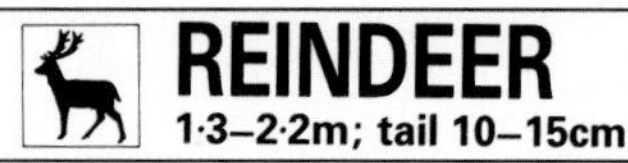

REINDEER

1·3–2·2m; tail 10–15cm *Rangifer tarandus*

♂

A large deer standing up to 1·2m at shoulder. Both males and females bear branched antlers. Coat variable, dark grey-brown to white. Patch of white on rump. Males bear a short mane of lighter hair under neck. Hooves broad.

Lives in herds, eating mainly lichen, moss, grass, twigs and shoots. It is an important domesticated animal in the far north and truly wild reindeer are now rare in Europe. An expert swimmer and fast runner.

Its natural habitat is the northern coniferous forest and the tundra. Wild reindeer are still found in Iceland, southwest Norway and parts of Finland eastwards.

Elk; Red Deer.

ELK

Alces alces **2·5–2·7m; tail 4–5cm**

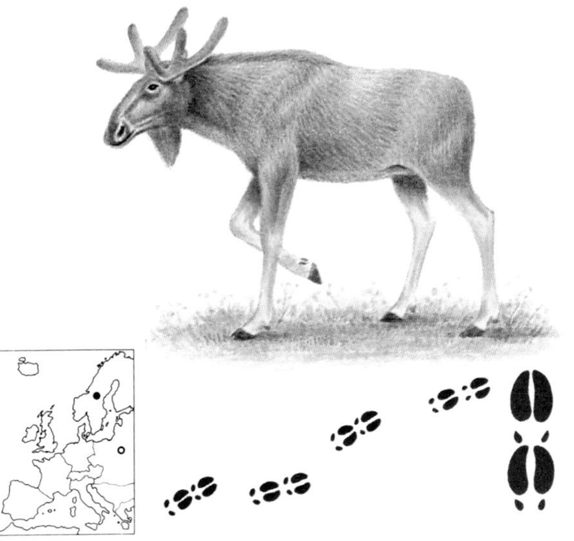

The largest European deer, standing up to 2·2m at shoulder and attaining a weight of up to 800kg (males). Prime males bear broad flat antlers. Dark brown coat with large tassel of hair under chin in males. Broad prominent nostrils.

Solitary or in small groups. Eats twigs and shoots of young trees, shrubby ground cover, and water plants. In the north seasonal migrations of thousands of animals take place from high grounds down to winter feeding grounds in forests.

Throughout Scandinavia eastwards through taiga, but also now spreading southwards and westwards into eastern European and Austrian forests.

Reindeer.

OTHER DEER

Sika Deer (*Cervus nippon*) (**1**). A medium-sized deer introduced from eastern Asia, spotted in summer, much darker and unspotted in winter. Males have a mane of thick hair and branched antlers. White rump patch bordered with black. Short tail with a black stripe. Sporadic distribution in wild in Britain, France and central Europe. Often kept in parks.

Muntjac (*Muntiacus reevesi*) (**2**). A tiny dark brown deer from China, little bigger than a fox. Male carries simple antlers and a pair of thin tusks in upper jaw. Introduced and established in wild in southern England in woodland.

Chinese Water Deer (*Hydropotes inermis*) (**3**). A small light brown deer introduced from China. Smaller than Roe Deer, larger than Muntjac. Neither males nor females have antlers. Male has long tusks in upper jaw visible from a distance. Grassland, open woodland in southeast England.

CHAMOIS

Rupicapra rupicapra **1·1–1·3m; tail 7–8cm**

A wild relative of sheep and goats, standing up to 80cm high at shoulder. Both sexes bear short permanent horns curved sharply back at tips. Broad black stripe down side of white face. Coat brown with black legs (summer) to black (winter).

Grazes during the daytime in alpine meadows around or above treeline, amongst steep rocky slopes. An agile climber. Large herds of females and young, with males living solitary. Alarm call a sharp whistle and also bleats like a goat.

In high mountains, chiefly the Alps, but also in Pyrenees and Carpathians and introduced elsewhere (e.g. the Vosges).

Ibex.

IBEX

1·3–1·5m; tail 12–15cm *Capra ibex*

A heavily-built goat, standing up to 85cm high at shoulder. Large horns in male curve backwards and are heavily ridged on flat front surface. Female has smaller horns. Coat grey-brown with paler belly. Uniformly coloured face.

Surefooted and agile on steep rocky terrain. Females and young form small herds, males are more solitary. Feeds on grass, dwarf shrubs, lichens, etc. Closely related to the wild goat, with which it can interbreed.

Lives high in mountains, typically higher than the Chamois. Found in Alps, Tatra Mountains of Czechoslovakia and in mountains in Spain.

Chamois: Feral Goats are lighter in build, often piebald with horns twisted or spiral. True wild goats which closely resemble the Ibex found in Crete and some Greek islands.

MOUFFLON

Ovis musimon

1·1–1·3m; tail 5–10cm

A relative of the domestic sheep, standing up to 75cm at shoulder. Male has large circular horns. Coat short haired, often piebald in males, with a mane of thicker hair at neck. Females smaller, no horns and brown coat. White rump patch.

Females and young live in flocks, males forming separate flocks for most of the year. Feeds principally at night on grass and sedges, resting in cover during the day.

In its native Sardinia and Corsica lives in steep mountain woods near treeline. Introduced into parts of France, Germany, Austria, northern Italy in woodland.

None.

EUROPEAN BISON

2·5–3m; tail 50–60cm *Bison bonasus*

A dark brown animal similar in size to a domestic cow, standing up to 1·95m high at shoulder, but with a heavier head and rougher coat. Adult males have a thick mane of longer hair on neck and shoulders. Both sexes have horns.

Lives in small herds in deciduous forest. It became extinct in the wild in the 1920s but was reintroduced from stock remaining in parks and zoos.

Small herds have been built up from introductions in eastern Europe, especially in the Bialowiecza forest in Poland, the home of the last wild herd.

None.

WILD BOAR

Sus scrofa

1·1–1·85m; tail 15–20cm

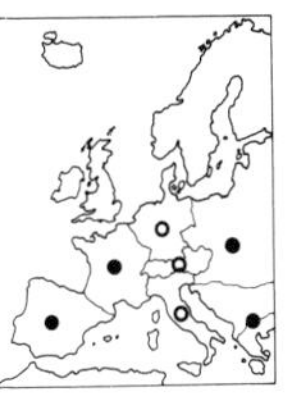

A heavy-bodied animal with large head and short legs. Dark brown coarse hair, with a bristly crest on neck and shoulders. Male has short curved tusks at corners of mouth. Piglets are light brown with longitudinal pale stripes.

Active mainly at night, sleeping in cover during the day. Omnivorous, taking acorns, beechmast, roots, earthworms and carrion. Warning cry is a short harsh grunt.

Throughout central and southern Europe in woodland and cultivated land where there is good cover, but has become extinct in heavily farmed areas.

None. Some old breeds of domestic pig resemble it in colour, but are shorter-haired and more 'pig-like'.

BARBARY APE

60–70cm; no tail *Macaca sylvanus*

Despite its name and lack of tail, the Barbary Ape is a monkey, closely related to the Rhesus monkey. It has a primate's typical long limbs with prehensile hands and feet, flattened face, forward-looking eyes and small ears.

A ground-living monkey, but is a skilful climber on rocky slopes. It feeds on all sorts of vegetable matter, insects and other small animals. Forms a hierarchical social group with a dominant male.

Dry rocky hillsides covered with scrub. In Europe only found on the Rock of Gibraltar where a half-tame group of 30–40 is maintained. Main range is in northern Africa.

None.

COMMON SEAL

Phoca vitulina

1·5m

Streamlined body with hind flippers turned inwards. Colour varies from grey to brown with dark spots on back, creamy with darker spots below. The face has a distinct forehead (compare Grey Seal) and short muzzle.

Generally lives in colonies on sand banks in sheltered harbours or estuaries and stays in shallow water. Eats a variety of fish. Pups usually grey brown and swim within a day or two of birth.

Around the coasts of the British Isles, the north coast of Spain and the Atlantic coast of France.

Grey Seal; **Ringed Seal**.

GREY SEAL

2·5m *Halichoerus grypus*

A large dark grey seal with a long muzzle and straight profile to face (compare Common Seal). Pattern of light and dark blotches. Males larger than females with heavy neck and shoulders with folds of blubber. Pups are white.

Lives around rocky coasts, breeding in crowded colonies on flat rocky shores and small islands. Travels considerable distances. Feeds mainly on fish. Noisy, making grunting and wailing ('singing') sounds.

Breeding colonies in Brittany, Britain and Ireland, the Faroes, Iceland, northern Norway and the Baltic. Individuals found around coast from northern Spain to the Baltic.

Common Seal.

MONK SEAL

Monachus monachus

3m

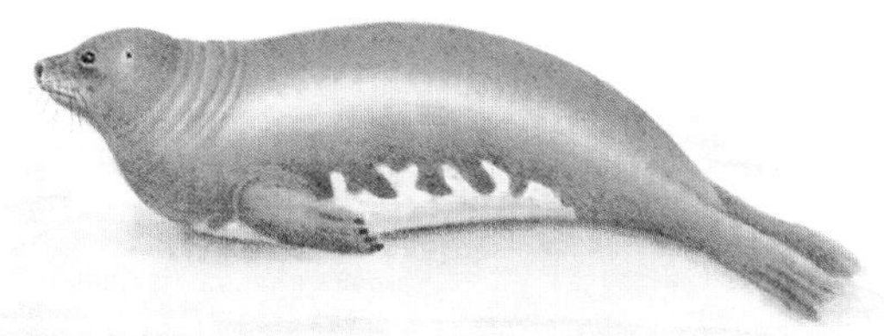

A large brown seal with variable white patch on underside. Pups black for first few weeks.

Breeding colonies on secluded sandy beaches, in caves or below cliffs.

Mediterranean, where it is now very rare due to development of its breeding sites, pollution and hunting by fishermen.

None.

RINGED SEAL

1·5m *Phoca hispida*

Very similar in size and markings to Common Seal but dark patches on back are ringed with lighter fur. Pups have a creamy white coat for first few weeks.

Lives in inshore waters or close to ice in Arctic and in the northern Baltic, keeping airholes open in ice in winter. Breeds on ice near land in spring.

In Europe, found on coasts of Iceland and Norway in winter, and in northern Baltic.

Common Seal.

COMMON DOLPHIN

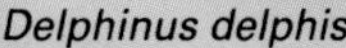

Delphinus delphis **up to 3m**

Sleek streamlined animal with a dark grey back, very light grey underside and a pattern of yellow and grey on sides. Dark 'spectacles' over eyes. It has a 'beak' about 15cm long.

Forms large schools and may be seen rolling and leaping in the sea, often diving in unison, or riding bow waves of ships. Dolphins have teeth and catch fish like sardines and herring and also squid.

Mediterranean and warmer parts of Atlantic, often coming north to the English Channel and sometimes further.

Bottle-nosed Dolphin; **Rough-toothed Dolphin**; **Porpoise**; **White-beaked Dolphin**.

BOTTLE-NOSED DOLPHIN

up to 4m *Tursiops truncatus*

Generally light to medium grey all over with a paler underside. A large dolphin, with a short beak, high pointed dorsal fin and a groove separating the beak from forehead.

Seen usually in small groups of 10 to 20 swimming and rolling in the sea, often with just back and dorsal fin showing, sometimes leaping out of the water. Feeds on various fishes. This is the dolphin that usually performs in dolphinaria.

Coastal waters from the Black Sea and Mediterranean north to the North Sea.

Common Dolphin; **Porpoise**; **Rough-toothed Dolphin**; **White-beaked Dolphin**.

ROUGH-TOOTHED DOLPHIN

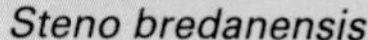

Steno bredanensis **2m**

A small dolphin, black above and white below, with pale irregular spots on side. The pronounced elongated beak runs smoothly into forehead.

A sociable species, forming groups of up to 50 and sometimes playing in the bow waves of ships.

Lives in tropical Atlantic waters, its range extending as far as the Mediterranean. Rarely seen further north.

Common Dolphin; **Bottle-nosed Dolphin**; **Porpoise**.

WHITE-BEAKED DOLPHIN

3m *Lagenorhynchus albirostris*

A large dolphin, black above, white underneath with a complicated lighter pattern on side and a white beak. Back fin large and pointed.

A very gregarious species sometimes forming schools of over a thousand members. Migrates from polar waters to warmer areas in spring to breed, making smaller groups. Feeds on fish, including herring and cod.

North Atlantic, North Sea, sometimes coming as far south as the Portuguese coast.

Common Dolphin; **Bottle-nosed Dolphin**; **Porpoise**.

PORPOISE

Phocoena phocoena up to 1·8m

Small compared to a dolphin and rather dumpy, with a small, blunt dorsal fin. Has no beak. Black above and white below.

Usually seen in small groups in bays and estuaries. Slower swimmer than a dolphin and does not leap clear of the water. Feeds on fish, crustaceans and cuttlefish.

Coastal waters from northern Europe to Mediterranean and Black Sea. Rare in Mediterranean and declining in North Sea and around British Isles due to pollution.

Dolphins have beaks.

KILLER WHALE

Up to 9m (male) *Orcinus orca*

A toothed whale with a large triangular dorsal fin (up to 2m long in adult males). Distinctive pattern of black back and white underside, with white patches extending backwards on each side behind the flipper, and a white eye patch.

Nomadic, living in family groups of up to 40. It is a hunter, taking seals, sharks and smaller fishes, small whales and porpoises, but is not dangerous to man. Becomes very docile in captivity and can be trained.

Worldwide distribution, in cool but not icy waters. Ranges throughout European waters from Iceland to the Mediterranean.

The rarely seen False Killer Whale is black all over and has no beak.

LONG-FINNED PILOT WHALE

Globicephala melaena **Up to 8m**

A large toothed whale, with a large curved fin on back and a bulbous forehead. The beak is small. Long pointed flippers. Black all over except for a patch of white between flippers.

A sociable species occurring in schools of around 20 to 100 swimming close to the surface. Feeds mainly on cuttlefish and squid. This is the whale hunted in the traditional Faroese hunt.

In European waters most numerous around Iceland, the Faroes and Shetland. Comes as far south as the Mediterranean, often close inshore.

The Bottle-nosed Whale, which also has a bulbous forehead, has a longer beak and smaller back fin. Most common around Iceland and Norway, migrates into British waters late summer.

WHITE WHALE

up to 5m *Delphinapterus leucas*

A distinctive small whale, white all over when adult, with a rounded head and body, flippers with upturned tips and no dorsal fin. Calves are blue grey.

Lives in small groups of females and calves or young males together, but migrates in larger herds. Feeds at the bottom in shallow waters on shrimps, crabs and fishes.

An Arctic species, living around the ice and in coastal waters. Occasionally wanders south to the North Sea and English Channel.

None.

SPERM WHALE

Physeter catodon

up to 18m (males)

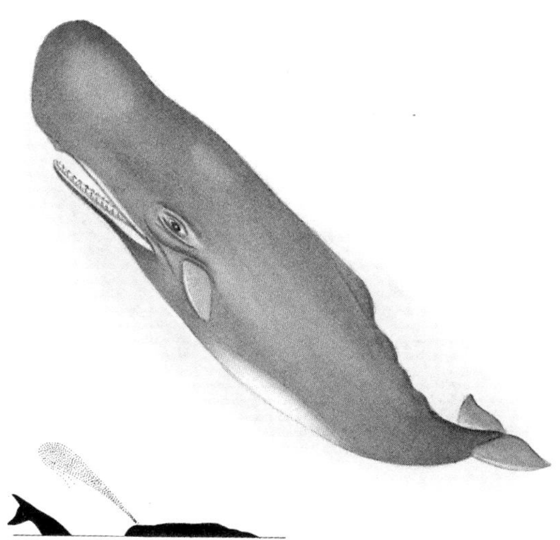

A large whale with a huge blunt head and narrow, toothed lower jaw. It is a dark bluish grey, has small flippers and no true dorsal fin, only a series of 'humps'. Females are smaller than males.

Lives in groups of 30 or more, either females and calves or young males together. Characteristic left-handed spout blows at 45°. Feeds on deep water animals, giant squid and fishes. Numbers in serious decline from hunting.

Worldwide distribution in tropical and warm temperate waters. Migrates to polar waters in summer. Has been found in Mediterranean.

The Humpback Whale is a different shape with long whitish flippers and expanding vertical spout.

SOWERBY'S WHALE

5m *Mesoplodon bidens*

A small beaked whale, with an elongated snout and all black or paler below. Often with pale scratch marks on the skin. Male has a single pair of tusk-like teeth in lower jaw.

Rarely seen in coastal waters but has been found stranded. Seems to live in pairs.

North Atlantic, has been found stranded chiefly on southern Scandinavian and North Sea coasts.

Of other beaked whales the Bottle-nosed Whale is larger (up to 9m) with a bulbous forehead, seen off Iceland, Norway and in British waters, and used to be hunted.

FIN WHALE

Balaenoptera physalus **up to 20m**

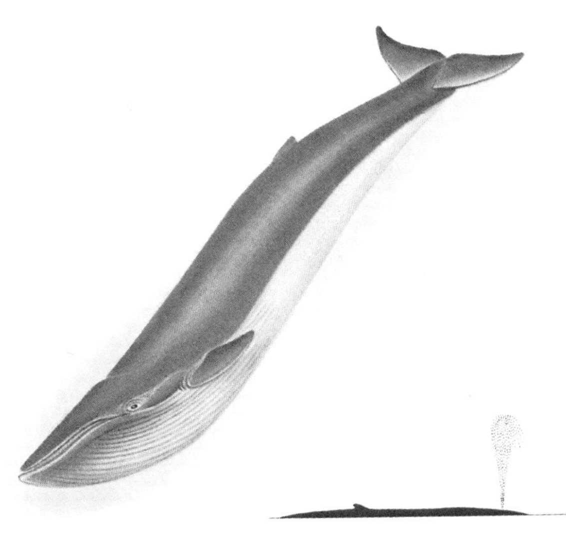

A large baleen whale, with a dark body above and white below, the white coming right up to the mouth and tip of snout on the right side only. Throat deeply furrowed. Small dorsal fin towards tail end.

A gregarious species, feeding near the surface on 'krill', a small crustacean it strains out from the water through the baleen plates in its mouth, and small fishes.

Worldwide in temperate and polar waters. In Europe, around Iceland, Faroes and Norway, migrating into British waters in late summer, and in western Mediterranean.

Sei Whale.

SEI WHALE

up to 18m *Balaenoptera borealis*

A large baleen whale similar to the Fin Whale but thicker bodied and with a larger dorsal fin. Symmetrical white underside to head.

Usually solitary or in pairs. Feeds on small crustaceans.

Worldwide distribution in temperate and polar waters. In Europe, sometimes seen around Iceland in summer. Rarely seen further south.

Fin Whale.

MINKE WHALE

Balaenoptera acutorostrata **up to 10m**

One of the smallest baleen whales. Black back with white underside and characteristic white band across flipper. Deep furrows on throat.

Usually seen alone or in small family groups. Feeds on small fish, crustaceans and small squid.

Worldwide distribution in temperate and polar waters. Found in all European waters from Arctic to Mediterranean, especially over the continental shelf.

Fin Whale and **Sei Whale** are much larger and lack the white band on flipper.

Index and checklist

Keep a record of your sightings by ticking the boxes.